Read-Alouds and Performance Reading:

A Handbook of Activities for the Middle School Classroom

Read-Alouds and Performance Reading:

A Handbook of Activities for the Middle School Classroom

by

Christine Boardman Moen

Christopher-Gordon Publishers, Inc.
Norwood, Massachusetts

Copyright Acknowledgments

Christopher~Gordon Publishers, Inc.
Bridging Theory and Practice

1502 Providence Highway, Suite #12
Norwood, Massachusetts 02062

800-934-8322
781-762-5577

Printed in the United State of America
10 9 8 7 6 5 4 3 2   07 06 05

ISBN: 1-929024-74-6
Library of Congress Catalogue Number: 2004100008

Dedication

To Dr. Marrietta Castle, a fellow "reading warrior"
with whom I am honored to
serve on the Board of Directors of the
Illinois Council for Affective Reading Education.

If we teach a child to read, yet develop not the taste
for reading, all of our teaching is for naught.

—Charlotte Huck, 1973, p. 305*

---

*Strategies for Improving Interest and Appreciation in Literature. In A. Berry, et al. (Eds).
Elementary Reading Instruction: Selected Materials (2nd ed.). Boston, MA: Allyn and Bacon.

Contents

Preface

Read-Alouds and Performance Reading: A Handbook of Activities for Middle
School Classrooms is a "theory-into-practice" book for teachers just start
ing out in the demanding yet immensely rewarding profession of teaching. At the same time, it's a "best practices" book that experienced teachers can
use to get new ideas and freshen up "tried but tired" ones already in place.

Each chapter is a "mini-book" unto itself with its own research base and dedicated routines, so if you're interested in just a few of the topics, you don't need
to read the entire book in one sitting. Chapter 1 is dedicated to the wide body of
research that supports the use of read-alouds and performance reading in the
classroom. Chapters 2, 3, and 4 are dedicated to three types of performance
reading: Readers Theater, Performance Poetry, and Storytelling. Performance
reading is a read-aloud routine that is teacher-modeled but primarily student-
centered because it involves students performing pieces of literature through
oral interpretation. Chapters 5, 6, 7, and 8 are devoted to read-alouds that are
more teacher-centered. The topics for these chapters include read-alouds dedicated to picture books, musical literture, informational texts, as well as novels
and short stories.

Because each chapter is dedicated to one specific read-aloud or performance
reading routine, the general guidelines that I follow appear below. Some are
common-sense but others require planned intention before they become ha-
bitual. The list is not ordered according to importance; each guideline contributes to an over-all successful teacher-presented and/or student-presented
read-aloud or reading performance.

Finally let me add that the myriad of routines described in this book are ones I have used and continue to use with my middle school students. I've developed these routines over the years as I have taught and continue to teach different age groups at the middle school level. The most significant premise of this book is that you, as a middle school classroom teacher, should establish a regular read-aloud or performance reading activity in your daily classroom schedule. What I am not suggesting is that you should you try to do every single routine in this book with all of your students within the framework of one school year. Therefore, I urge you to select the routines that fit your teaching style and the needs of your students, and use them on a regular basis.

Ten To-Do's for Successful Read-Alouds and Performance Reading Routines

1. Establish regular routines that fit your teaching style and classroom setting. By establishing regular routines, you demonstrate to your students that read-alouds and performance reading are valuable uses of time and activities that are not just "add-ons."

2. Establish a purpose for every read-aloud or performance reading and make sure your students know it. This includes acquainting students with any information they will need prior to the read-aloud or performance reading so they can be intelligent, active listeners.

3. Preview and prepare every read-aloud and performance reading even if it's one you've done many times before. In other words, your read-aloud or performance reading should be a well thought-out part of your lesson plan.

4. Read a variety of materials—long, short, fiction, nonfiction.

5. Begin the read-aloud or performance reading only when everyone is ready to listen and everyone is seated wherever you or they wish to be seated.

6. Decide and explain the type of student response you wish from your students before beginning the read-aloud or performance reading.

7. Whenever possible, provide extra copies of your read-aloud or performance reading text for those students who want and need to have a copy so they can follow along.

8. Make connections between the various read-alouds and performance readings you share throughout the year.

9. Read aloud and encourage your students to read aloud with expression and animation.

10. Keep records of the material you designate to be used for your read-aloud and performance reading routines and always be on the lookout for new material to add to your program.

With purpose, preparation, and planning, you can establish read-aloud and performance reading routines in your classroom that will motivate your students and improve their reading skills.

Chapter Summary Guide

The table of contents provides you with a quick "snapshot" of what you will find in each chapter; however, if you have a bit more time and/or are looking for a specific topic, you'll find these chapter summaries useful.

Chapter 1—"Reality and Reconciliation: Making the Case for Regular Read-Aloud and Performance Reading Routines in the Middle School Classroom"

Since current classroom practices must be "research-based" and "standards-aligned," you'll find a significant amount of research to support your decision to use read-alouds and performance reading routines on a daily basis. The routines in this book can help students improve their vocabularies, comprehension, and fluency—important reading skills addressed by the National Reading Panel's report upon which much of the No Child Left Behind legislation is based. Just as importantly, you'll find research that describes how motivational read-alouds are to students, and how they can have a positive impact on students' desire to read independently.

Chapter 2—"Readers Theater: Performance Reading as a Read-Aloud Routine"

Readers Theater is a type of read-aloud routine in which students present a piece of literature as a performance. Although the literature is performed, traditional theater requirements such as costumes, props, and special lighting are not used. Students discuss the literature selection with their cast members to ensure comprehension and to improve fluency and oral expression through multiple readings. Scripts are most often created through the adaptation of different literature selections such as short stories, chapter books, and picture books, although at times you may have students create original scripts. Different purposes for the use of Readers Theater as a performance reading routine are described. A resource list of novels, chapter books, short stories, picture books, and folk tales is provided as is a grading rubric for a Readers Theater performance.

Chapter 3—"Performance Poetry: Lifting Poetry Off the Page and Into the Hearts and Minds of Students"

Performance Poetry is a type of student-presented read-aloud routine that is a blend of poetry and stagecraft. Performance Poetry is similar to Readers Theater in that the use of costumes, props, and special lighting are not encouraged. Comprehension, vocabulary, fluency, and oral expression are the targeted skills. Seven types of poetry performances are described. A poetry reading log, performance rubric, student performance preparation sheet, and a list of suggested poems are also provided.

Chapter 4—"Storytelling: Student + Audience = Literacy"

This chapter describes how storytelling can be used as a performance reading read-aloud routine. Rationale and research to support the use of storytelling in the classroom are provided as well as detailed descriptions detailing how to implement, manage, and assess this type of performance reading. A storytelling log sheet, tip sheet, and grading rubric are provided as well as an extensive list of different types of stories suitable for middle school students.

Chapter 5—"Picture Book Read-Alouds: Affective and Effective Literacy Entry Points"

Several reasons for the use of picture books at the middle school level are given and supported with research as is a list of criteria for choosing appropriate picture books for use with middle school students. Also supplied is a description of how to share a picture book in a middle school setting where class size often exceeds 30 students. Two picture book student-response categories are identified: entertaining/intriguing picture books and picture books that can be connected or somehow related to longer chapter books. A student-response graphic organizer is provided to use when the teacher reads aloud an entertaining/intriguing picture book. A different student-response graphic organizer is provided to use when the teacher reads aloud picture books that can be connected to longer chapter books which can be offered to students as choices for their independent reading. A list of suggested picture books as well as picture books tied to chapter books is provided.

Chapter 6—"Musical Read-Alouds: Combinations That Hit the Right Notes"

Music is a powerful tool that can enhance students' literacy learning. Music can help students focus their thinking and help increase the amount of attention they invest in a piece of literature. In addition, music can help students create a first-person emotional connection to a literature selection. Practical suggestions describe how to coordinate and catalog a repertoire of musical literature pieces. Specific titles of books and stories along with suggested musical selections are provided to help teachers implement this exciting, new read-aloud category.

Chapter 7—"Nonfiction: The Function, Form, and Finesse of the Informational Text Read-Aloud"

The notion that fiction is for read-aloud and nonfiction is for research is debunked. Research supporting the use of nonfiction for read-alouds is described, and criteria for selecting informational text is provided. Five different nonfiction text patterns are described and key identifying words listed. Five different types of student-response graphic organizers are provided as well as a list of books that can be used for each type of informational text read-aloud.

Chapter 8—"Novels, Short Stories, and Short Pieces: The Long, the Short, and the Very Short Read-Aloud"

This chapter begins with a suggested criteria for selecting novels and short stories for classroom read-alouds. In addition, a brief description is supplied that explains how to help students acquire the background knowledge they will need prior to their using the three different types of student-response graphic organizers entitled "Make a Connection," "Language Lifts," and "See What I Hear." Cataloging suggestions are given; and a list of novels, short stories, and short pieces is provided.

Chapter

1

Reality and Reconciliation:

Making the Case for Read-Aloud and Performance Reading Routines in the Middle School Classroom

When it comes to my own classroom, I take the concept of "theory into practice" very seriously. As a professional classroom teacher, it is my responsibility to assess "new trends" or "hot topics" as some journals label them and to decide whether the trends or topics are merely fads or are suggested practices so fabulous that I adopt them—and adapt them—to work in my own classroom.

The teachers I know, who are reflective practitioners and who understand that teaching is a blend of art and science, operate the same way. We sift the "wheat from the chaff"; and we do it very quickly because we are busy, dedicated individuals. And because I recognize you as a busy, dedicated individual, I promise not to keep you away from your students and your busy schedule for too long as I attempt to explain *why* various types of read-alouds belong in your classroom, *how* you can easily implement them, and *what* resources you might use with each type.

Reality

In most classrooms, time is the enemy. There's never enough. While we usually can't change the amount of time we have with our students, we do have control over what we do with that time. And with more required state and possibly national testing on the horizon, we must adopt classroom practices that are broad enough to connect with all learners in our classroom yet narrow enough to positively affect students' skills and strategies as well as their achievement on assessment tests. The reality is that using various types of read-alouds and performance readings in our classrooms can result in such a "broad yet narrow" practice.

Reading-Alouds Are Motivational

Our students are often as busy as we are. In fact, many students identify themselves as "dormant readers"—students who are able to read but declare that they don't have time to read (Beers, 1998). These dormant readers will become nonreaders if they are not exposed to reading and are not given time to read in class. *Learning to Read in Our Nation's Schools*, a report by the National Assessment of Educational Progress (Langer, Applebee, Mullis, Foetsch, 1990), reveals that as students move into middle school and then into high school, they read for pleasure less, own fewer books, and visit the library less. Furthermore, Guthrie, Alao, and Rinehart (1997), as well as Ryan and Patrick (2001), report that as students reach the middle school, their intrinsic motivation for literacy and other academic subjects declines. Moreover, as these students move into the intermediate grades and beyond, their teachers read aloud to them less until only a small percentage of teachers read aloud daily to their students (Jacobs, Morrison, & Swinyard, 2000) and (Langer, Applebee, Mullis, & Foertsch, 1990). The bottom line is that our students are reading less outside of school, and we middle school teachers are reading aloud to them less than when they were in elementary school.

We all know that people "find the time" to do things they enjoy doing. We also know that people usually get better at an activity when they engage in it frequently. Consequently, we teachers need to motivate students to read by reading aloud to them and by giving them opportunities for performance reading. Then we need to allow them to practice their reading independently by giving them time to read in class.

Why read to them and then give them time to read? First, Livaudais (as cited by Lesesne 1991) reports that teacher read-alouds are motivational to seventh through twelfth graders, and Krashen (1993) reports that story read-alouds promote independent reading. My own classroom experience echoes what Atwell (1987) reports about good read alouds: Students are attentive during read-alouds, and they are motivated to borrow the books used in read-alouds as well as motivated to seek out books written by the same author (p. 208). Ivey (2002) also reported that teacher read-alouds motivate students to read the same book on their own. Echoing the motivating factor of read-alouds is Sanacore (1996, p. 589) who contends that "carefully chosen materials we read aloud today are likely to be read by our students tomorrow." In addition, Lesesne (1998, p. 251) in describing her own experiences states, "one of the most powerful ways to turn around disinterest is by reading aloud to students."

As for giving students time to read in class, your students are probably like mine and like the students about whom Hollis Lowery-Moore (1998, p. 33) describes in "Voices of Middle School Readers." When Lowery-Moore interviewed students, they "noted the importance of giving them the opportunity to read during school." Gardiner (2001) makes the modest proposal of allowing students to read silently for 10 minutes daily. Gardiner (2001, p. 34) further notes, "In a typical sustained silent reading program, most middle school students can read about 1 million words and learn about 1,000 new words each year without any direct instruction in vocabulary." And does practice make perfect? Perhaps not perfect, but there is a correlation between the amount of leisure reading students engage in and their reading achievement scores. Anderson, Wilson, and Fielding (1983) discovered that children who scored at the 90th percentile on a reading test spent five times as many minutes per day reading books as children who scored at the 50th percentile. In addition, the Reading to Learn Institute at the San Diego County Office of Education (1996) states in its report that "reading promotes reading—the more they [students] read, the more their vocabulary grows, the more words they can read, the more reading they can do." It can be difficult to "give up the stage" after a teacher read-aloud because we feel like we should be "doing something." However, the reality is that when we allow students to read independently during class time, we *are* doing something.

Read-Alouds Positively Impact Students' Reading Skills

Vocabulary acquisition, the application of comprehension strategies, text structure recognition, and fluency—these are some of the goals of a balanced literacy program; they are also areas that state reading assessment tests attempt to measure. Although not the *only* classroom practice that should be used to teach these skills, using a variety of read-alouds and performance reading is a recommended practice and is one that can introduce, teach, and reinforce these important reading skills and strategies.

A student's reading vocabulary doesn't catch up to his or her listening vocabulary until the student reaches college age (Sticht, 1974, and Loban, 1963, as cited by Chall, 1983). Trelease (2001, p. 9) refers to a student's listening vocabulary as "the reservoir of words that feeds the speaking vocabulary, the reading vocabulary and the writing vocabulary—all at the same time." In addition, Stahl (1999) concluded that older students' vocabularies benefited from listening to read alouds and Allen (2000, p. 47) contends that read alouds help students build an awareness of the reading components of "reading motivation, word knowledge, syntax, story grammar, genre knowledge, authors' intentions, readers' choices, and understanding." Additionally, the National Reading Panel (2000), whose report influenced the No Child Left Behind (NCLB) legislation, addressed the issue of vocabulary instruction and determined that students can learn vocabulary "in the context of storybook reading or in listening to others" and also found helpful the practice of vocabulary instruction prior to reading—an important instructional activity that should precede any read-aloud.

The National Reading Panel (2000) also addressed the topics of comprehension and fluency. The Panel cited Harris and Hodges' (1995, p. 39) definition of comprehension as "intentional thinking during which meaning is constructed through interactions between text and reader." Reading aloud to students can affect students' comprehension. First, Porter (1969 as cited by Butler 1980) found that reading aloud to fourth, fifth, and sixth graders affected their comprehension achievement. Furthermore, Teale (1984) found that read-alouds helped students become aware of text and how written language works. Additionally, a meta-analysis done by Martinez (1989 as cited by Lesesne 1998) on research done on reading aloud to students in grades kindergarten through 12 showed that students who were read to showed gains in reading comprehension and vocabulary, and showed gains on sentence structure and usage tests. Finally, the NRP determined that some of the types of instruction that worked to improve comprehension included instruction that involved:

✓ comprehension monitoring

✓ cooperative learning

✓ the use of graphic and semantic organizers

✓ questioning and answering by students and teachers

✓ summarizing

✓ instruction related to story structure for the purpose of story recall

Because NCLB and NRP are related, I did an analysis of the Panel's types of effective comprehension instruction and aligned them with the read-aloud routines set forth in this book as a way of showing that a variety of teacher and student performance readings can support comprehension instruction in the classroom.

- Read-alouds should require students to respond through summarization.

  Summarizations through:
  - Short story retellings
  - Storytelling rehearsals
  - Sentence summarizations of nonfiction text

- Read-alouds should utilize graphic and semantic organizers.

  Utilizing organizers through the use of:
  - AlphaFacts, Succinct Sentences, and others with nonfiction text
  - Make a Connection, Language Lifts and others for fiction

- Read-alouds should emphasize story and text structure.

  Emphasis of story structure through:
  - Storytelling, Novels, Short stories, Readers Theater, Poetry Performance, Picture books, and Musical Literature

  Emphasis of text structure through:
  - Cause-effect, comparison-contrast, problem-solution, chronological, and enumeration text patterns in nonfiction and informational texts

- Read-alouds should incorporate student and teacher questions and answers.

  Incorporating student and teacher questions and answers through:
  - Selection, preparation, and performance during Storytelling, Performance Poetry, and Readers Theater
  - Literacy connections between picture books and novels
  - Connections between music and literature

- Read-alouds should involve students learning to read together.

  Students learning together during:
  - Storytelling, Performance Poetry, and Readers Theater
  - Short story and nonfiction response activities
  - Listening to read-alouds as a learning community

- Read-alouds should support students' comprehension monitoring.

  Comprehension monitoring through:
  - Responses to fiction and nonfiction
  - Preparation for Storytelling, Performance Poetry, and Readers Theater.

One final note: The NPR reported that if the comprehension instruction they cited are used in combination, "these techniques can improve results in standardized comprehension tests."

Just as comprehension can be improved through read-alouds, student performance reading can help improve fluency. Although fluency seems to be difficult to define, we recognize when a student is not a fluent reader. The components of fluency include the student's rate, accuracy, and automaticity of word recognition as well as the smoothness, phrasing, and expressiveness with which the student reads (Worthy & Broaddus, 2001–02). Fluency is important in reading because fluent readers have a more positive attitude toward reading and have a more positive attitude about themselves as readers (Rasinski & Padak, 2000). Fluency is also tied to comprehension (National Reading Panel, 2000).

Repeated readings (which are absolutely essential for such performance reading as Performance Poetry, Storytelling, and Readers Theater) work to improve fluency in a wide range of students (Samuels, 1979, 2002) and also lead to improved comprehension (Hasbrouck, Ihnot, & Rogers, 1999). Oakley (2003) reported improved fluency with the students in her study who were required to prepare, rehearse, and perform their text in a similar fashion in which students prepare, rehearse, and perform Storytelling, Readers Theater, and Performance Poetry read-alouds. Also, students need to hear fluent reading in order to read fluently themselves (Clark, 1995), and read-alouds can provide such models of fluency for students. Moreover, listening to a fluent reading model enables students to "store 'model voices' in their heads"(Oakley, 2003, p. 5). With such stored models, students can compare the models to their own oral reading performances and make adjustments and improvements. Finally, repeated readings can lead to fluency that can be transferred to new material that students are asked to read without prior rehearsal (Dowhower, 1987).

Just as importantly, research shows that read-alouds have an impact on two growing student populations: unskilled, unmotivated readers, who are hostile toward reading and who find reading "boring," and dialect-speaking students, who are unfamiliar with standard American English (Sanacore, 1996).

Unskilled, unmotivated readers approach reading as a process of figuring out words. To the unskilled, unmotivated reader, reading is a skill that is required to get through school. Because these students "don't hear or see anything as they read," reading is "boring" (Beers, 1996, p. 111). Furthermore, reading is confusing to the unskilled, unmotivated reader and, therefore, she or he is unable to make any personal connections or responses to it. However, a teacher read-aloud can provide an "in-common text experience" (Davidson & Koppenhaver, 1993, p. 186) where all students from the gifted reader to the unskilled reader are able to discuss and respond to the same text thereby becoming members of the "literacy club" (Smith, 1985, p. 2). According to Lesesne (1991, p. 63) "Read-alouds can effectively build a response community within the classroom." Just as important, read-alouds give students access to books they cannot read independently (Mooney, 1990) and provide opportunities for students to derive personal, cultural, and academic benefits (Vail, 1977, as cited by Butler, 1980). Furthermore, a teacher read-aloud can help unskilled readers (and sometimes skilled readers as well) understand confusing text. Ivey (2003, p. 812) reports that read-alouds make "otherwise difficult text interesting and comprehensible." As Lesesne (1998, p. 251) explains, students "do not want us to read books aloud; they want us to act them aloud." This "acting books aloud" using different inflections, hand movements, volume, and pace aides students' understanding. In my own classroom when students comment that a particular passage is confusing, I read the passage aloud so they can recognize who is speaking and the tone in which they are speaking. Or if the passage is descriptive, I read it aloud while students attempt to draw or create a picture in their heads as to what the author is describing.

Finally, Sanacore (1996, pp. 590–591) discusses demographic trends and societal pressures as they relate to lifelong learners and the role of read-alouds. Sanacore notes that many students come from homes where both parents work or come from homes where a single parent must work. As a result, many students' after-school activities involve watching television, talking on the telephone, and a myriad of activities other than reading. In addition, Sanacore notes "a growing number of students who speak a dialect of English." With both groups of students, Sanacore recommends read-alouds because "it [reading aloud] can instill a love of reading and thereby create within learners a desire to develop the lifetime literacy habit." As for dialect-speaking students, read-alouds can be used to "increase [the] learners' familiarity with standard American English since it represents the vast majority of text that they will experience."

For the most part, the type of read-aloud discussed thus far has been the teacher read-aloud. In subsequent chapters, student-centered performance readings such as Readers Theater, Storytelling, and Performance Poetry will be discussed in detail and supported with research that explains their impact on fluency, understanding of text structure, comprehension, vocabulary, confidence, motivation, and other literacy skills such as listening and speaking. These student-centered oral performances provide alternate as well as additional ways to view read-alouds and their impact on student motivation, independent reading, and reading skills.

Reconciliation

Despite all of the information I have provided you as to why read-alouds should be a part of your classroom's balanced literacy program, I urge you to do one additional task to convince yourself that regular read-alouds belong in your classroom. You need to reconcile the benefits and likely outcomes of read-alouds with the goals and standards your district and your state expect you to follow and your students to achieve.

Most states have adopted or are in the process of adopting state standards for each of the content areas. For example, the state in which I currently live has adopted a set of English Language Arts standards which include several goals and performance descriptors. One overall state goal in English Language Arts addresses the skills of listening and speaking in various situations. One of the learning objectives listed under this broad goal specifies that students must demonstrate ways that active listening can improve comprehension. In my classroom, read-alouds and performance reading are ideal ways to help students achieve this goal. Another overall state goal in the content area of English Language Arts is reading and understanding a variety of different types of literature from various cultures and time periods. A learning objective under this goal indicates that as a result of reading a variety of literature, students should be able to explain how characters handle conflict and solve problems. Furthermore, students should be able to explain how these skills can be applied to real-life situations. Again, I use read-alouds to help my students achieve this goal. And finally, when the state goal indicates that students should be able to read fluently and accurately materials that are appropriate for their age, I use student-presented read-alouds to help them achieve this goal (ISBE, 2002, p. 5, 12, 18).

Beyond an examination of your state standards, you may want to review the "Standards for the English Language Arts" established by the International Reading Association and the National Council of Teachers of English (IRA & NCTE, 1996). Teacher and student read-alouds help meet and exceed a number of these standards including students being able to:

✓ Apply a "wide range of strategies to comprehend, interpret, evaluate, and appreciate text."

✓ Read a "wide range of print" including "fiction, nonfiction, classic, and contemporary works."

✓ Adjust their use of "spoken, written, and visual language" for a "variety of audiences and for different purposes."

✓ Read a "wide range of literature from many periods in many genres."

✓ Apply "knowledge of language structure" including figurative language.

✓ Participate as "knowledgeable, reflective, creative, and critical members of a variety of literacy communities."

I could continue the list. Instead, I invite you to perform the "reconciliation test." See for yourself how using read-alouds in your classroom will help you meet the standards. I think you will discover that using a variety of read-alouds in your classroom will help you pass the (reconciliation) test with flying colors!

References

Allen, J. (2000). *Yellow brick road: Shared and guided paths to independent reading 4–12.* Portland, ME: Stenhouse.

Atwell, N. (1987). *In the middle: Writing, reading, and learning with adolescents.* Portsmouth, NH: Boynton/Cook.

Anderson, R., Wilson, P., & Fielding, L. (1983). Growth in reading and how children spend their time outside of school. *Reading Research Quarterly, 23,* 285–303.

Beers, K. (1998). Choosing not to read: Understanding why some middle school students just say no. In K. Beers & B. Samuels (Eds.), *Into Focus: Understanding and creating middle school readers* (pp. 37–63). Norwood, MA: Christopher-Gordon.

Beers, K. (1996). No time, no interest, no way! Part II. *School Library Journal, 42* (3), 100–113.

Butler, C. (1980). When the pleasurable is measurable: Teachers reading aloud. *Language Art,* November/December, 882–885.

Chall, J. S. (1983). *Stages of reading development.* New York: McGraw-Hill.

Clark, C. H. (1995). Teaching students about reading: A fluency example. *Reading Horizons, 35*(3), 250–266.

Davidson, J., & Koppenhaver, D. (1993). *Adolescent literacy: What works and why,* 2nd ed. New York: Garland.

Dowhower, S. L. (1987). Effects of repeated reading on second-grade transitional readers' fluency and comprehension. *Reading Research Quarterly, 22,* 389–406.

Gardiner, S. (2001). Ten Minutes a Day for Silent Reading. *Educational Leadership, 59,* 32–35.

Gurhrie, J., Alao, S., & Rinehart, J. (1997). Engagement in reading for young adolescents. *Journal of Adolescent and Adult Literacy, 39* (6), 436–445.

Harris, T. L., & Hodges, R. E. (1995). *The literacy dictionary: The vocabulary of reading and writing.* Newark, DE: International Reading Association.

Hasbrouck, J. E., Ihnot, C., & Rogers, G. H. (1999). Read Naturally: A strategy to increase oral reading fluency. *Reading Research and Instruction, 39* (1), 27–37.

Illinois State Board of Education (2002). English language arts performance descriptors grades 6–12. Retrieved January 19, 2003, from http://www.isbe.state.il.us.

Ivey, G. (2002). Getting started: Manageable literacy practices. *Educational Leadership, 60* (3), 20–23.

Ivey, G. (2003). The teacher makes it more explainable and other reasons to read aloud in the intermediate grades. *The Reading Teacher, 56* (8), 812–814.

IRA & NCTE. (1996). *Standards for the English language arts.* Newark, DE: IRA and Urbana, ILL: NCTE.

Jacobs, J., Morrison, T., & Swinyard, W. (2000). Reading aloud to students: A national probability study of classroom reading practices of elementary school teachers. *Reading Psychology, 21,* 171–193.

Krashen, S. (1993). *The power of reading: Insights from the research.* Englewood, CO: Libraries Unlimited.

Langer, J. A., Applebee, A. N., Mullis, I. V. S., & Foertsch, M. A. (1990). *Learning to read in our nation's schools: Instruction and achievement in 1988 at grades 4, 8, and 12.* Princeton, N.J.: National Assessment of Educational Progress and Educational Testing Service.

Lesesne, T. (1991). Developing lifetime readers: Suggestions from fifty years of research. *English Journal,* October, 61–64.

Lesesne, T. (1998). Reading aloud to build success in reading. In K. Beers & B. Samuels (Eds.), *Into focus: Understanding and creating middle school readers* (pp. 245–260). Norwood, MA: Christopher-Gordon.

Lowery-Moore, H. (1998). Voices of Middle School Readers. In K. Beers & B. Samuels (Eds). *Into focus: Understanding and creating middle school readers* (pp. 23–35). Norwood, MA: Christopher-Gordon.

Mooney, M. (1990). *Reading to, with, and by children.* Katonah, NY: Richard C. Owens.

National Reading Panel (NPR). (2000). *Teaching children to read: An evidence-based assessment of the scientific research literature on reading and its implications for reading instruction.* Bethesda, MD: National Institute of Child Health & Human Development, National Institutes of Health. Available at www.nichd.nih.gov/publications/nrp/report.htm (Retrieved July 2003).

Oakley, G. (2003, March) Improving oral reading fluency (and comprehension) through the creation of talking books. *Reading Online, 6* (7). Available at http://www.readingonline.org/articles/art_index.asp?HREF=oakley/index.html (Retrieved June 2003).

Rasinski, T., & Padak, N. (2000). *Effective reading strategies: Teaching children who find reading difficult* (2nd. ed.). Upper Saddle River, NJ: Merrill.

Reading to Learn Institute. (1996). *Free voluntary reading: Theory into practice monograph.* Retrieved January 19, 2003, from http://www.sdcoe.k12.ca.us.

Ryan, A. M., & Patrick, H. (2001). Peer groups as a context for the socialization of adolescents' motivation, engagement, and achievement in school. *Educational Psychologist, 35,* 101–111.

Samuels. S. J. (1979). The method of repeated readings. *The Reading Teacher, 32* (4), 403–408.

Samuels, S. J. (2002). Reading fluency: Its development and assessment. In A. E. Farstrup & S. J. Samuels (Eds), *What research has to say about reading instruction* (pp. 166–183). Newark, DE: International Reading Association.

Sanacore, J. (1996). An important literacy event through the grades. *Journal of Adolescent and Adult Literacy, 39* (7), 588–591.

Smith, F. (1988). *Joining the literacy club.* Portsmouth, NH: Heinemann.

Stahl, S. (1999). *Vocabulary development.* Cambridge, MA: Brookline.

Teale, W. (1984). Reading to young children: Its significance for literacy development. In J. Goelman, A. A. Oberg, & F. Smith (Eds), *Awakening to literacy* (pp. 110–121). London, England: Heinemann.

Trelease, J. (2001). *The read-aloud handbook.* New York: Penguin Books.

Worthy, J., & Broaddus, K. (2001–02) Fluency beyond the primary grades: From group performance to silent, independent reading. *The Reading Teacher, 55* (4), 334–343.

Chapter 2

Readers Theater:

Performance Reading as a Read-Aloud Routine

Being old enough to actually have used Coger and White's (1973) *Readers Theatre Handbook* as a college text, I can attest that Readers Theater has been a popular activity in speech and drama classes and then in English and language arts classrooms for quite some time. However, because of its adaptation for elementary classrooms, Readers Theater is currently experiencing an exciting surge in popularity. And with its popularity in elementary classrooms, Readers Theater is also being revitalized in middle school classrooms as well. Below are definitions and explanations of Readers Theater from the 1970s, 1980s, 1990s, and from 2001:

> Basically, Readers Theatre is a medium in which two or more oral interpreters through vivid vocal and physical clues cause an audience to see and hear characters expressing their attitudes toward an action so vitally that literature becomes a living experience—both for the readers and for their audience. (Coger & White, 1973, p. 4)

> Readers Theatre is a medium involving group reading of a literary script focusing on dialogue between two or more delineated

characters who, through voice and bodily tension rather than movement, cause the audience to sense imaginatively characterization, setting, and action. (Latrobe & Laughlin, 1989, p. 3)

Readers theater is a group project that involves the reading of a prepared script based upon a literary work. Typically, the actors sit on stools or chairs in the front of the room and read the scripts; there is little, if any, movement involved as character is developed by dialogue rather than other means such as gesture and costume. (Beers & Samuels, 1998, p. 256)

Readers Theater is a presentation by two or more participants who read a script. The focus is on an effective reading of the script rather than on a memorized presentation with body movements, elaborate staging, props, and costumes. Readers may stand behind music stands that hold their scripts or sit on stools, chairs, or the floor. One or more narrators may read introductory material and provide background information not conveyed through the characters' readings. (Barchers, 2001, p. 11)

If we compile the common essential elements from all four definitions from the past 30 years, Readers Theater, which is a student-centered performance reading, involves the following:

✓ Students work individually to create a character but work as part of a group to create a complete performance reading.

✓ Students read from a script which they write or which has been prepared specifically for the Readers Theater performance reading.

✓ Students do not use props, lighting, costumes or any other theatrical device but instead stand or sit facing the audience.

✓ Students' dramatic, oral readings are essential to the effectiveness of this read-aloud approach.

There are several meaningful benefits of Readers Theater as a student-centered read-aloud. First, because Readers Theater requires students to prepare for the presentation by reading the script multiple times, Readers Theater has a positive impact on fluency (Blau, 1999). Cunningham and Allington (2003) support the use of repeated readings to improve fluency; however, Readers Theater has a distinct advantage in the area of repeated readings because students read the script multiple times for the authentic literacy purpose of preparing a performance for an audience. As stated in *Put Reading First*, a booklet published by the U.S. Department of Education (Armbruster, Lehr, & Osborn, 2001, p. 29), "Readers Theater provides readers with a legitimate reason to re-read text and to practice fluency." In addition, because students closely interact with text by analyzing it, performing it, and sometimes writing it themselves, they practice metacognitive skills (Kelleher, 1997) which are tied to comprehension. Not only does Readers Theater require students to comprehend the text but it also requires students to cooperate and to work together to practice and perform (and sometimes write) their text. And having students learning to read together is a suggested "best practice" by the National Reading Panel (2000), a report upon which the No Child Left Behind legislation is partially based. Finally, Readers Theater is motivational (Millen & Rinehart, 1999), a fact to which I can attest with a personal anecdote. One day before class started and while I was counting out Readers Theater scripts, I casually asked one of my notoriously reluctant readers why she always volunteered to read in our Readers Theater presentations. She enthusiastically replied, "It's [Readers Theater] not really reading. It's fun!" To this student and other aliterate students—students who can read but choose not to—reading from a book, especially a textbook, is boring, but with Readers Theater, the text "comes to life."

Because the text "comes to life" through each reader's oral expression, struggling readers benefit from participating and listening to Readers Theater performances. For example, my struggling readers often get lost in a text when they can't follow who is talking during dialogue exchanges. These students simply aren't able to make the switch back and forth and keep the characters straight unless the author uses tags like "she said" and "he said" when each character speaks. However, after a Readers Theater presentation, my struggling readers "light up" with understanding because they are able to see and hear the dialogue exchanges and recognize who said what.

One final benefit of Readers Theater that I've experienced in my own classroom is that Readers Theater has allowed me to give recognition and opportunity to students who aren't "in the mainstream." Because early in the year I have students read aloud to me privately while I do an oral reading miscue analysis (Goodman, Watson, & Burke, 1987; Woods & Moe, 1999), I am able to note which students have pleasing read-aloud voices. So often, the students who have the most interesting and desirable voices are the students who are socially "on the fringe." Usually, however, I am able to coax and to cajole these students into participating in Readers Theater, and once they find success and acceptance—at least in my classroom during that brief time doing Readers Theater—she or he is hooked and becomes a regular volunteer.

A casual classroom Readers Theater presentation.

Using Readers Theater
for a Variety of Purposes

Readers Theater is a highly adaptable student-centered read-aloud, and I use it in a variety of ways in my classroom.

Sales Pitch for Independent Reading

Trelease (2001, p. 8) contends "reading aloud serves as a commercial for the pleasures of reading." I agree, and this is why I use Readers Theater as a commercial for books I want to "sell" to my students for their independent reading choices. Secondly, I use Readers Theater to "sell" a core book I want my entire class to read. An example of using Readers Theater to sell a book for independent reading choice is Avi's book *Wolf Rider* (Simon & Schuster, 1986), which in my opinion, serves as the model for the best three "grabber" introductory pages written for a young adult novel. These are the first three lines of the book:

> The kitchen phone rang three times before Andy
> picked it up. "Hello?" he said.
> A voice replied, "I just killed someone."

The suspense builds and listeners and readers are left wondering if the call is a prank or if someone has actually killed a girl named Nina. After a trio of readers performs the first three pages of the book, which I transformed into a Readers Theater script, the book zips off my classroom library shelves throughout the school year. I usually end up having to buy a new copy of the book every other year.

An example of the way in which I use Readers Theater to get my students excited about reading a "core" book, which is a book I require all of my students to read, is Christopher Paul Curtis' book *The Watsons go to Birmingham—1963* (Delacorte, 1995). Just as I believe Avi's book serves as a model for "grabber" introductory pages, I believe Curtis' first chapter is a model "grabber" introductory chapter. Every time I use Readers Theater to introduce this novel, my students insist on reading for the remainder of the class period. Or as one student recently politely but firmly said to me, "Mrs. Moen, could you be quiet now, so we could read?" Given such a cue, I promptly closed my mouth, got out the pillows, turned on some soft "reading" music, and read right along with the students.

Picture Book Read-Alouds

I use a variety of picture books in my classroom, and one way I use them is to provide fun, easy-to-prepare Readers Theaters. The picture books that I use for Readers Theater usually rely on sophisticated humor or have more mature themes than most easy-to-read picture books used in many elementary schools. An example of a picture book that my students love to perform as Readers Theater is Margie Palatini's and Richard Egielski's *The Web Files* (Hyperion, 2001), which is a wacky satire of the old *Dragnet* television series. (Note: This book is an excellent example of the need to introduce topics prior to students reading a text. Before rehearsing the script I wrote based on this picture book, I have my students listen to old radio shows of *Dragnet*. By hearing the old scripts, the students appreciate the dry humor and the use of such sound effects as "Dum De Dum Dum.")

Easy Chapter Book "Read Arounds"

Easy chapter books such as Jon Scieszka's *Time Warp Trio* books (Puffin, 1993), Sid Fleischman's *The Whipping Boy* (William Morrow, 1986) and, my favorite, Natalie Babbitt's *The Search for Delicious* (Farrar, Straus, & Giroux, 1969) make excellent Readers Theater selections. Different student groups prepare assigned chapters, rehearse, and perform the chapters in the order in which they appear in the book. It's an easy and enjoyable way for students—especially struggling readers—to read entire books.

Short Story Enhancements

Short stories, folk tales, and fairy tales are wonderful ways to get students comfortable with Readers Theater. These materials are usually easy to adapt, and you can have several different performances within one class period allowing many students the opportunity to read aloud. In addition to picture books, I use short stories extensively at the beginning of the school year so students quickly understand the concept of Readers Theater and get comfortable using it as a type of performance reading.

End of Novel Scenes

One final way I use Readers Theater is to have students select a scene from a novel the class has read or a book their literature circle group has read and transform it into a Readers Theater performance reading. For example, when my students finish reading Lois Lowry's *The Giver* (Houghton Mifflin, 1993), I ask them to select groups, choose a scene, transform the scene into a Readers

Theater script, rehearse it, and perform it for their peers. It's a wonderful way to end the unit, and the Readers Theater read-aloud provides me with an alternative way to assess my students' understanding of the text.

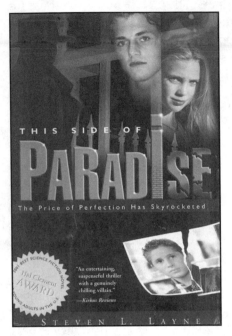

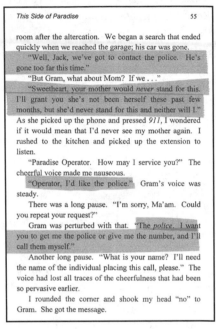

This Side of Paradise by Steven L. Layne, Pelican, 2002.

Script preparation using removable highlighter tape (used by permission).

Preparing Readers and Preparing Scripts

I do not have students adapt literature for their own Readers Theater scripts until they have had ample opportunities to observe and participate in numerous Readers Theater read-alouds. First, I want students to enjoy reading aloud, to practice reading with expression, and to develop a sense of community spirit by performing in front of their classmates. I want my students to *want* to read, because I believe if I establish this *affective* objective as the centerpiece of my reading program, my students' reading skills will improve, too. With this in mind, my "deadline" for having students adapt literature for their own scripts is the end of October. This is a convenient time to eat Halloween candy and have a "Creep Festival" of scary stories presented as Readers Theater read-alouds.

There are numerous sources which offer guidelines for selecting and adapting materials for Readers Theater, and there are numerous sources of ready-made scripts. For ready-made scripts, I rely on *Read* magazine, which is published by the Weekly Reader Corporation. Additional resources appear at the end of this chapter, and I urge you to check them out. However, what I'd like to share with you here are the "nuts and bolts" of what I do.

Preparing the Picture Book, Short Story, or Complete Chapter

1. Each student must have a copy of the text. With short stories, I usually enlarge the type and photocopy each page so each page can be taped onto construction paper to avoid "rattling pages" during performances. Picture books are expensive, so I have one copy per group and copies of the typed version of the text for each group member. When I use chapter books for the foundation for scripts, each group member has a copy of his own.

2. Students use highlighters to mark their short story and picture book texts following the guidelines below:

   • Each script must have at least one narrator who helps establish the place, time, and sequence of events in the story.

   • The tag lines ("he said") are crossed out on the script.

   • Descriptive scenes can be condensed and rewritten. (I don't go high-tech. Students simply rewrite the section on a piece of paper and tape it in place on the script.)

   • A character can be eliminated from the story if the elimination does not affect the overall story.

   • Students are encouraged to write themselves "expression reminders" and to add them to their scripts in parenthesis (e.g., whispers, sad). This reminds students to follow the expression cues and to read the script as indicated.

3. Students use highlighter tape (available in school supply stores) to mark their parts on the pages in their chapter book, and the tape is removed after the performances. (See example on previous page.)

   • The text is not altered except for the elimination of tag lines.

Preparing a Scene to Sell the Book or as an End-of-Book Activity

1. Each student must have a copy of the text.

2. Using the evaluation criteria that appear in Figure 2.1, each student selects **two possible scenes** from the book and brings the completed criteria sheets to the group's first meeting. A reminder: Each member in the group must have a speaking part even if it is only a few lines.

3. Groups discuss the scenes and select one to present.

4. The scripts as well as the introduction and conclusion to the scene are crafted during group meetings (usually two to three). A script is word processed outside of class by one group member and kept on disk. Characters' lines are typed as follows:

> MANUEL: Did Alex ask you for a ride to the soccer match?
>
> TY: Yes! Can you believe that after what he did to me in practice?

The group has a "read through" of the preliminary script and the group makes any changes. Changes to the script are made on disk and copies of the final script are printed. Pages are taped to construction paper and collated or hole-punched and put into a three-prong folder.

5. Students rehearse their parts on their own but are given class time to rehearse as a group. (I usually schedule rehearsal time so each group practices twice each class period over the course of 2 or 3 days depending upon students' schedules and attendance.)

Name _____

Title _____ Scene pages _____

Think of your selected scene as a short story. Give your scene a short story title:
_____

Name the characters in the scene (include the narrator) _____
_____

Explain this scene's importance as it contributes to the overall story presented in this book. (In other words, what makes this scene stand out from others?) _____
_____
_____

Each scene must have a beginning, a middle, and an ending. Your group will have to write an introduction to explain how the scene fits into the book's storyline, and your group will have to write a conclusion to "wrap up" the scene. Be prepared to tell your group how the scene you selected is an example of a "slice of life" from the book and how the scene will fit between an introduction and conclusion.

If you are selecting a scene to "sell" your book, explain how your scene will arouse interest without giving away too much of the story. _____
_____

If you are selecting a scene to "sell" your book, your introduction will have to include a brief description of the characters in the scene. Write those brief descriptions below:

Character 1 _____

Character 2 _____

Character 3 _____

Figure 2.1   Scene Selection Criteria

Evaluating the Readers Theater Performance

The only time I evaluate a Readers Theater performance is when the students prepare the script and perform a chosen scene to either sell a book or as an end-of-book activity. *I never give group grades.* Instead, each group member is graded to assess his or her contribution to the success of the project. A sample of my grading rubric appears in Figure 2.2.

The other student-centered Readers Theater read-alouds are stress-free. Students do them as part of the class's overall performance reading routine. Students know this is pleasure reading (and I know that they are working on their reading skills.)

Readers Theater is a student-centered read-aloud that can improve a student's motivation to read as well as his or her fluency and comprehension. Given these benefits, Readers Theater is a wise use of classroom reading instruction time.

Name _____

Title of Book or Scene _____

Copy of Student's Script is Attached   Yes (5)   No (0)

Detail on Criteria Sheet 1   Outstanding (4)   Significant (3)   Adequate (2)   Minimal (1)

Detail on Criteria Sheet 2   Outstanding (4)   Significant (3)   Adequate (2)   Minimal (1)

Student Response:

Explain two specific ways you contributed to your group's Readers Theater Read-Aloud:

Scene Selection (4)   Script Preparation (4)   Group Rehearsal (4)

1. _____

_____

2. _____

_____

Teacher Observation of Performance:

Individual Rehearsal Is Evident:

Outstanding (10)   Very Good (8)   Adequate (7)   More Needed (6)

Group Rehearsal Is Evident:

Outstanding (10)   Very Good (8)   Adequate (7)   More Needed (6)

Final Comments: _____

_____

_____

Total Points out of 45 _____ Letter Grade _____

Figure 2.2   Readers Theater Scoring Rubric

Resources

Books Formatted for Readers Theater

The following books lend themselves to Readers Theater because they are stories told from multiple viewpoints. They require a minimal amount of script preparation.

Witness by Karen Hesse (Scholastic, 2001)
Life changes for the eleven characters in this small Vermont town. The year is 1924, and the Ku Klux Klan has decided to move in.

Nothing But the Truth: A Documentary Novel by Avi (Orchard, 1991)
The national media reports that a student is suspended from school for singing the national anthem. Through letters, diary entries, memos, and announcements as well as character dialogue, readers discover the truth and nothing but the truth of the entire incident.

Who Killed Mr. Chippendale? A Mystery in Poems by Mel Glenn (Lodestar Books, 1996)
A respected high school English teacher is shot during his morning run at the school track. Mr. Chippendale's life and death are examined through the eyes of a variety of people until, finally, his killer is revealed.

Bull Run by Paul Fleischman (HarperCollins, 1993)
In brief vignettes, 16 different people from the north and the south describe their participation in or connection with the Battle of Bull Run.

Seed Folks by Paul Fleischman (HarperCollins, 1997)
A cluttered city lot is transformed into a community garden by a diverse group of people, who end up growing friendships as well as fruits, vegetables, and flowers.

Short Books for Easy Chapter Adaptations

Each of the following books lends itself to Readers Theater because each contains a variety of interesting characters yet is short enough so the text can be highlighted as a script directly in each chapter of the book.

The Hundred Dresses by Eleanor Estes (Voyager Books, 1988)
Little Wanda Petronski lives in Boggins Heights and is the daughter of a Polish immigrant. She is taunted and teased by her classmates for wearing the same drab dress to school and declaring that she has a hundred dresses at home in her closet. Estes' classic serves as a reminder for today's students that teasing is painful.

Crash by Jerry Spinelli (Random House, 1997)
Crash Coogan is popular and is a star football player. Penn Webb is a vegetarian Quaker who goes out for the cheerleading squad. Both love their grandfathers and eventually become best friends.

It's All Greek to Me by Jon Scieszka (Puffin, 2001)
Part of the Time Warp Trio series, Fred, Sam, and Joe are whisked back to the time of the Greeks while rehearsing a school play about Mount Olympus.

Whirligig by Paul Fleischman (Random House, 1998)
Four separate stories are woven together, each tied to whirligigs built by Brent Bishop, a high school student who is doing penance and finding redemption for the vehicular manslaughter of an innocent teenage girl.

The Whipping Boy by Sid Fleischman (William Morrow, 1986)
When Prince Brat, who lives up—or down—to his name, is supposed to be punished, Jemmy is punished instead, for he is the prince's whipping boy. Jemmy attempts to escape and finds himself in a role-reversal with the prince and in the company of the villain, Hold-Your-Nose-Billy.

Later, Gator by Laurence Yep (Hyperion, 1995)
Family traditions and sibling rivalry are mixed with a pet alligator in this story that has fine dialogue for Readers Theater.

Short Stories, Picture Books, and Folk Tales

The Web Files by Margie Palatini and Richard Egielski (Hyperion, 2001)
Referred to earlier in this chapter, this picture book is a satire of the old *Dragnet* radio and television shows.

Epossumondas by Coleen Salley (Harcourt, 2002)
Lucky for this picture book's readers, Epossumonda doesn't have "the sense he was born with" as he brings home bread, butter, and even a puppy from Auntie's house.

"Testing" by Tamora Pierce in *Lost and Found* edited by M. Jerry Weiss and Helen S. Weiss (Tom Doherty, 2000)
The residents at the Smithton Home for Girls get yet another new housemother. They've managed to drive away the previous ones. Will Doreen Swanson be next or will she pass the girls' test?

"All Summer in a Day" by Ray Bradbury in *Children of the Future*, edited by Isaac Asimov (Raintree, 1984).
It rains all day, every day on the planet Venus, and the children in Margot's class have never seen the sun. But today is special. Today, the rain will stop and the sun will shine for one hour before it is hidden by the rain for another 7 years.

"How Many Spots Does a Leopard Have?" by Julius Lester in *How Many Spots Does a Leopard Have? And Other Tales* by Julius Lester (Scholastic, 1989)
  In the title story of this book, vain Leopard offers a prize to anyone who can count his spots for him since he doesn't know how to count. Others try to help until finally rabbit declares that Leopard has two spots—light and dark.

Additional Resources

Learning With Readers Theater by Neill Dixon, Anne Davies, and Colleen Politano (Peguis, 1996)

Introduction to Readers Theatre: A Guide to Classroom Performance by Gerald Lee Ratliff (Meriwether, 1999)

Center Stage: One Act Plays for Teenage Readers and Actors edited by Donald R. Gallo (HarperCollins, 1991)

Scary Readers Theatre by Suzanne I. Barchers (Teacher Ideas Press, 1994)

From Atalanta to Zeus: Readers Theatre From Greek Mythology by Suzanne Barchers (Teacher Ideas Press, 1997)

Frantic Frogs and Other Frankly Fractured Folktales for Readers Theatre by Anthony D. Fredericks (Teacher Ideas Press, 1993)

Stories on Stage by Aaron Shepard (H.W. Wilson, 1993)

Read published by Weekly Reader www.weeklyreader.com

References

Armbruster, B., Lehr, F., & Osborn, J. (2001). *Put reading first: The research building blocks for teaching children to read.* Jessup, MD: Center for the Improvement of Early Reading Achievement, Office of Educational Research and Improvement U.S. Department of Education.

Barchers, S. (2001). Enhancing reading with readers theater. *Knowledge Quest,* September 11.

Blau, L. (2001). Five surefire strategies for developing reading fluency. *Instructor, 110* (7), 28–30.

Coger, L., & White, M. (1973). *Readers Theatre handbook.* Glenview, Ill.: Scott, Foresman.

Cunningham, P., & Allington, R. (2003). *Classrooms that work.* Boston: Allyn and Bacon.

Goodman, Y. M., Watson, D. J. & Burke, C. L. (1987). *Reading miscue inventory: Alternative procedures.* New York: Richard C. Owen.

Kelleher, M. E. (1997). Readers theater and metacognition. *The New England Reading Association Journal, 33* (2), 4–12.

Latrobe, K., & Laughlin, M. (1989). *Readers theatre for young adults.* Englewood, CO: Teacher Idea Press.

Layne, S. L. (2002). *This side of paradise.* Gretna, LA: Pelican.

Lesesne, T. (1998). Reading aloud to build success in reading. In K. Beers & B. Samuels (Eds.) *Into focus: Understanding and creating middle school readers* (pp. 245–260). Norwood, MA: Christopher-Gordon.

Millin, S. K., & Rinehart, S. D. (1999). Some of the benefits of readers theater participation for second-grade Title I students. *Reading Research and Instruction, 39* (1), 71–88.

National Reading Panel. (2000). *Teaching children to read: An evidence-based assessment of the scientific research literature on reading and its implication for reading instruction. Reports of the subgroup.* Bethesda, MD: National Institutes of Health http://www.nichd.nih.gov/publications/nrp/.

Trelease, J. (2001). *The read-aloud handbook.* New York: Penguin.

Woods, M. L., & Moe, A. J. (1999). *Analytical reading inventory.* Saddle River, NJ: Merrill.

Chapter

3

Performance Poetry:

Lifting Poetry Off the Page and
Into the Hearts and Minds of Students

I've always enjoyed poetry, but until a few years ago, I knew I was not very successful at getting my students to enjoy poetry. My failure to infuse my students with the enthusiasm I felt for poetry was frustrating. I knew they picked up on my enthusiasm for other types of literature that I read aloud. Why not poetry?

Then I went to a literacy conference and saw a demonstration of Performance Poetry, and I finally realized what was wrong with my approach to poetry. I was reading poetry aloud, and I was having my students read it aloud, but I also was treating poems like dead words on a page and asking my students to bring them to life by telling me what the words meant. Using this approach, by the time we finished discussing and dissecting the words and ideas in a poem, my students not only didn't like the poem, they never wanted to see it, read it, say it, or hear it again! Happily, Performance Poetry rescued us.

Performance Poetry is a blend of poetry and stagecraft. Just as a theatrical production breathes life into a playwright's script, so, too, does Performance Poetry lift poetry off the page and into the hearts and minds of students. Performance Poetry is not a Poetry Jam or Poetry Slam where poets compete with each other. At the same time, the term "poetry dramatization" is not appropriate either because students do not "act out" a poem as much as they interpret a poem using the appropriate tone of vocal and bodily expressions. In its purest form, the only props allowed during Performance Poetry are chairs or stools. Everything else is suggested. Of course, allowing props and adding music or other forms of accompaniment are a matter of personal taste; however, I've found that when I've allowed students to use simple props, they tend to neglect the words of the poem in favor of practicing clever ways to use their props. Finally, in order to help students participate fully in appreciating poetry as literature and in order to utilize Performance Poetry as a read-aloud approach, students need to know the following:

✓ different ways poems can be performed

✓ questions to answer while selecting poems to perform

✓ how to prepare a poem for a performance

Different Ways Poems Can be Performed

Students (and you as well) can use Performance Poetry as a performance reading routine in a variety of ways. Two students could choose the same poem to perform, yet each student's performance would be unique. However, before students begin to create their own poetry performances, it's appropriate that they become familiar with some "basic" ways poems can be performed. Some of these basic ways are described below along with suggested poems for each of these types of performances.

Chorus Line

This type of performance is a good way to introduce your students to Performance Poetry because each student is supported by the entire class. The student chooses a poem with a repetitious line that the class members repeat in support of the student performer. I like to use *Jump Back, Honey: The Poems of Paul Laurence Dunbar* (Hyperion, 1999) because it's jazzy and students like to snap their fingers and "sing-talk" the line "Jump Back, Honey, Jump Back."

> *Life Doesn't Frighten Me* by Maya Angelou (Stewart, Tabor, Chang, 1993)
>
> *Whoever You Are* by Mem Fox (Harcourt Brace, 1997)
>
> "Music" by Moises Reyes. Translated by Gabriela Kohen in *Movin' Teen Poets Take Voice*, edited by Dave Johnson (Orchard Books, 2000)

Class Act

Narrative poems as well as ballads work well with this type of performance that gets the entire class involved. It should be noted that Class Act is the closest Performance Poetry comes to "acting out" a poem. My favorite poem to use when demonstrating the Class Act type of performance reading is Ernest Lawrence Tayer's classic poem, "Casey at the Bat." Students take various parts and even the audience becomes part of the performance as the fans at the ball park.

> "The Highwayman" by Alfred Noyes
>
> "Paul Revere's Ride" by Henry Wadsworth Longfellow

Partner Poems

As the name implies, two people take different lines and perform a poem. I like to use Paul Fleischman's *Joyful Noise: Poems for Two Voices* (Harper, 1988) to introduce the idea of two voices because students can easily hear as well as easily see how the poem divides into two parts. Once they see the interplay that can occur between two people performing the same poem, I like to use other poems such as Nikki Grimes' "Hair Prayer" from *A Dime a Dozen* (Dial, 1998).

> "Honeybees" by Paul Fleischman in *Joyful Noise: Poems for Two Voices* (Harper&Row, 1988)
>
> "A Close Encounter" by Chris Gibson in *You are Here This is Now* Edited by David Levithan (Scholastic, 2002)
>
> "Start Me Up" by Janet S. Wong in *Behind the Wheel* (Simon & Schuster, 1999)

Many Voices

Poems that lend themselves to more than two people but not to an entire class fall into this category, thus making this a wide and deep category, indeed! To demonstrate this type of performance, I like to use Charles R. Smith Jr.'s ' "Everything I Need to Know in Life, I Learned from Basketball" from his book *Rimshots* (Puffin, 1999) because students can memorize their few lines quickly, and the poem requires a lot of basketball action. (I once had a class that consisted almost entirely of boys, so I used Rudyard Kipling's "If." I've learned that if I look hard enough and keep track of the poems I read, I can usually find a poem to fit almost all of my classroom needs.)

> *Colors* by Ken Nordine (Harcourt, 2000)
>
> *Jump Ball: A Basketball Season in Poems* by Mel Glenn (Lodestar, 1997)

Going Solo

Poems that lend themselves to individual performances run the gamut between Shakespeare and Silverstein with a little Robert Frost, Jack Prelutsky, and Emily Dickinson thrown in. The student who chooses to perform a poem by himself or herself usually has some type of attachment to the poem she or he has chosen. It's the student who brought me a copy of a poem she had found while surfing the internet and declared that she "must do this poem because it's so neat!" (The poem turned out to be Robert Frost's "Stopping by Woods on a Snowy Evening.") Or the student who gave a flawless performance of several lines from Lewis Carol's "Jabberwocky" to an astonished group of peers who cried out, "How did you ever memorize a poem like that?" She replied, "I grew up with that poem. My dad says it all the time!" These are the students who will choose a poem for Going Solo.

> *In Flanders Fields* by John McCrae, edited by Linda Granfield (Doubleday, 1995)

> "Losing It" by Sara Holbrook in *I Never Said I Wasn't Difficult* (Boyds Mills, 1996)

Novems

Novem is a blend of the words *novel* and *poem*. Thus a novem is an extended story told through a series of poems. A good example is the Newbery Honor book *Carver: A Life in Poems* by Marilyn Nelson (Scholastic, 2001). Using a novem for a poetry performance can be challenging yet rewarding. One way to tell an entire story through the use of poems is to first read aloud the entire book and then have students select poems to perform from the beginning, middle, and ending of the book. In this way, students will have the entire book as a context for their performance. Other novems such as those written by Mel Glenn are excellent for Readers Theater, while still others such as Sharon Creech's delightful *Love That Dog* (HarperCollins, 2001) are best presented as teacher read-alouds.

> *Out of the Dust* by Karen Hesse (Scholastic, 1997)

> *Carver: A Life in Poems* by Marilyn Nelson (Front Street, 2002)

> *My Man Blue* by Nikki Grimes (Dial, 1999)

> *Love That Dog* by Sharon Creech (HarperCollins, 2001)

> *Shakespeare Bats Cleanup* by Ron Koertge (Candlewick, 2003)

Poem-ologues

A poem-ologue is comparable to a soliloquy in a theatrical production. Rather than tell a story in verse like a novem, a poem-ologue is a collection of poems that support a topic or theme. A good example of a poem-ologue is the 14 poem collection in *Lives: Poems About Famous Americans* (HarperCollins, 1999). Poem-ologues lend themselves to a class presentation of various poems based on a theme which can be tied to other areas of your curriculum.

We the People by Bobbi Katz (Greenwillow, 2000)

Animals That Ought to Be by Richard Michelson (Simon & Schuster, 1996)

My America: A Poetry Atlas of the United States edited by Lee Bennett Hopkins (Simon & Schuster, 2000)

Selecting Poems to Perform

Because I require my students to read a lot of poetry before selecting one to perform, I use a log sheet with 20 entries like the one that appears in Figure 3.1.

Name _____

Title of Poem _____

Name of Poet _____

Book Title of Poem's Location _____

Page Number _____ Number of Lines in Poem _____

Mood of Poem: Silly   Excited   Sad   Lonely   Wistful   Scary   Other _____

Performance Ideas _____

Figure 3.1   Poetry Log Sheet

Students keep track of the poems they've selected; and once they have logged 20 poems, they conference with me and we decide which poem they will perform. In addition, we discuss the steps they will take to prepare their poem and also discuss the grading rubric, which appears in Figure 3.2.

Name_____

Volume and Pronunciation

_____(4) Outstanding speaking volume and pronunciation, natural-sounding
_____(3) Very easy to hear and understand speaker
_____(2) Able to hear and understand speaker
_____(1) At times difficult to hear and understand speaker

Vocal Expression

_____(4) Outstanding with attention to detail
_____(3) Demonstrated an excellent understanding of the poem
_____(2) Varied, demonstrated a good understanding of the poem
_____(1) At times lacked expression to adequately convey meaning of poem

Gestures and Movement

_____(4) Outstanding blend of gestures and movement
_____(3) Enhanced the performance
_____(2) Varied, added to the performance
_____(1) At time lacking and/or inappropriate

Preparation and Overall Performance

_____(4) Dynamic performance
_____(3) Demonstrated excellent preparation and performance flow
_____(2) Demonstrated adequate preparation and performance flow
_____(1) At times performance was halting and/or unrehearsed

Student(s)

began performance facing front with hands at his/her side.   Yes (1)   No (0)
ended performance facing front, hands at his/her side and bowed.   Yes (1)   No (0)
stated title of poem   Yes (1)   No (0)
stated poet's name   Yes (1)   No (0)

Additional Comments:

_____

_____

Score out of 20_____   Letter Grade_____

Figure 3.2   Performance Poetry Grading Rubric

There are two reasons why I require my students to log the poems they have read and are considering to perform. First, it forces students to keep reading poetry because so often they want to choose the first poem they read. Secondly, the log sheet is beneficial because occasionally a student will be unhappy with his selected poem once he starts rehearsing. Having the list allows the student to choose a different poem easily and get back to the task of preparing the poem for performance.

When considering a poem and deciding whether or not to record it on their log sheet, students use the following list of statements:

- I have read this poem twice.

- If someone asked, I could explain why I like this poem.

- I have read other poems by this poet OR I would like to read other poems by this poet.

- I understand what this poem is about OR I would like to talk to someone to help me understand what this poem is about.

- I think I would be able to memorize this poem.

- I have some ideas about how I'd like to perform this poem.

- I am willing to work alone, work with a partner, or work with others to rehearse this poem.

Prepaing a Poem for Performance

Once a student has selected a poem and we've talked about it, I give the student a copy of the poem and a preparation sheet like the one that appears in Figure 3.3.

Name_____

Directions: Follow the instructions below, to prepare your poem for performance. Check off each instruction after you've completed it.

_____ Go through the poem line by line and make sure you understand the meaning and pronunciation of each word including the author's name and the title of your poem.

_____ Highlight the punctuation in the poem and note the line breaks.

_____ Close your eyes and picture in your head what is happening in this poem.

_____ Underline any words that tell about the actions that take place in your poem.

_____ Using your background knowledge and any word cues from the poem itself, decide where your poem takes place. (This is the setting.)

_____ Identify the words or lines in the poem that help you recognize the mood of the poem.

_____ Think about how you will convey this mood with your facial expression, gestures, and your posture. Indicate these on your poem.

_____ Mark any parts of the poem where you or others will need to say words louder, softer, faster, or slower.

Figure 3.3   Performance Poetry Preparation Sheet

_____ If you are working with a partner or a group of students, indicate the lines you will say and the lines others will say. (Don't forget narrator, if you use one.)

_____ Indicate on your poem when and where you or others will move during the performance. If it is helpful, make a drawing in the margin of your poem or on a separate piece of paper.

_____ If the poem rhymes, practice saying the poem into a tape recorder so you can avoid using a "sing-song" delivery. Remember to talk instead of recite.

_____ When you rehearse, make sure you practice your beginning and your ending. At the beginning, all performers stand in a line facing the audience with hands at their sides. After the performance is over, all performers reform a line, and with hands at their sides, they take a bow.

_____ Record a rehearsal schedule below. Begin by writing in the date you will be performing and then work backwards. Give yourself classroom time as well as time outside of class. If you have other students who will be performing with you, make sure you inform them of your rehearsal schedule and post your schedule on the class bulletin board.

Name_____ Poem_____

Monday	Tuesday	Wednesday	Thursday	Friday
				15 Min. in Class
				Outside of Class (Indicate Time)

Figure 3.3   Performance Poetry Preparation Sheet *(Continued)*

There are a variety of ways you can schedule Performance Poetry. First, you can schedule a performance or a few performances during your daily read-aloud time. Scheduling this way requires that different students be prepared on different days, which has its advantages and disadvantages. It's advantageous because each performance is spotlighted. On the other hand, it can be disadvantageous because the more days the performance schedule covers, the chances increase that students will be absent and/or forget portions of their poems. Another way to schedule Performance Poetry is to have half the class perform on one day and the other half the next day. Finally, if everyone gets to perform in the classroom, you may want to ask students to volunteer to perform their poems for other classes in your school. After all, memorizing, staging, and rehearsing a poem for only one performance, even if that performance is videotaped, seems almost anticlimactic.

Poet Percy Bysshe Shelley (1840) said, "Poetry lifts the veil from the hidden beauty of the world, and makes familiar objects be as if they were not familiar."

Performance Poetry will not only "lift the veil," your students' performance readings will "bring down the house"!

Additional Resources

Books

Wham! It's a Poetry Jam by Sara Holbrook (Boyd Mills, 2002)

Handbook of Poetic Forms edited by Ron Padgett (Teachers & Writers Collaborative, 1987)

How to Write Poetry by Paul B. Janeczko (Scholastic, 1999)

Something Is Going to Happen: Poetry Performance for the Classroom by Allan Wolf (Poetry Alive! Publications, 1990)

Web Sites

Academy of American Poets   www.poets.org/wtnfrmst.htm
This site has a Real Audio "listening book" that presents poets reading their work.

Poetry Alive!   http://poetryalive.com
This site offers teacher resources for Performance Poetry.

Online Poetry Classroom   www.onlinepoetryclassroom.org
This site includes 12,000 poems along with biographies and other information on more than 450 poets.

Reference

Shelley, P. B. (1840). *A defence of poetry.* Retrieved November 1, 2003, from http://www.bartleby.com.

Chapter 4

Storytelling:

Student + Text + Audience = Literacy

I began seriously to think about storytelling as a performance reading routine after encountering a fourth grade student by the name of Zach, who agreed to be part of a cross-age reading group I'd assembled in the public elementary school my son was attending at the time. The purpose of the group was to have the struggling fourth grade readers prepare a picture book to read aloud to kindergartners who had been identified by their teacher as needing more "lap reading" time.

The cross-age reading group was a win-win situation. The fourth graders practiced fluency and gained confidence as readers by reading a variety of books and by reading each chosen book multiple times. In addition, students developed a good sense of when to stop and pose questions to their listeners. At the same time, the kindergarten students got to listen to more stories and had the opportunity to be with older readers.

Zach, who loved baseball and art class, did well reading to the kindergarten students, but he was resistant to the reading skills lessons required in his classroom. If Zach read a story from his basal and took a test, he failed it. If Zach read a story and wrote about it in his journal, it was impossible to follow what he had written. One day, I observed Zach drawing, and I asked him about one of the picture books he'd read for the cross-age reading group. Without even realizing it, Zach began to draw and tell the story. It was then I realized that Zach was a storyteller!

The experience with Zach led me to make the connection to Crockett Johnson's delightful stories of Harold as I recalled the story of *Harold and the Purple Crayon* (Scholastic, 1959). In all of Harold's adventures, he draws the story as it unfolds—just as Zach had done during my observation. As a result of meeting Zach and making the connection to Harold, I devised a storytelling technique I call "Crayon Conversations," which appears in my book *Better Than Book Reports* (Scholastic, 1992).

Having no formal training in storytelling, "Crayon Conversations" was my first attempt at using storytelling when I returned to classroom teaching a few years after meeting Zach. Now after much reading, practicing, and experimenting, I can confidently say that storytelling is a performance reading routine that is an important part of my read-aloud program.

Storytelling is a "complex and vibrant interactive experience" (Turner & Oaks, 1997, p. 154) that involves three elements: the story, the storyteller, and the audience (Colwell, 1983). Moreover, storytelling is "the act of crafting a literary document in public and in the process making language patterns and literary structures visible in ways no other experience can" (Moir, 1994, p. 57). But does storytelling, which according to storyteller Helen Forest (2000) offers the listener an opportunity to "design costumes, sets and scenery in the theatre of the mind," correlate with student achievement? Like other read-aloud and performance reading routines mentioned in this book, storytelling does lead to student achievement in a number of different areas.

Like other read-alouds, storytelling provides students with an in-common literacy experience that all can share regardless of reading ability. Additionally, storytelling allows "each child [to have] his or her own unique vision of the story characters and setting . . . as they naturally begin to imagine and make sense of the story while they listen" (Farrell, 1991, p. 12–13). This "visual thought" (Farrell, 1991) also describes why storytelling can help students develop a sense of scaffolding (Searle, 1984) or a type of cognitive framework (Nessel, 1985) that helps students understand and remember what they have read.

Trostle and Hicks (1998, p. 128) discovered that students who were exposed to stories told by adult storytellers using the "character imagery storytelling method" in which the storyteller uses gestures, body movement, and different voice intonations for individual characters scored higher on measures of comprehension and story vocabulary than those students who were exposed to adult story reading of the same literature selections. I cite this study not to discourage teachers from reading aloud. On the contrary, I cite it to underscore the need to use storytelling as an additional method for classroom read-alouds and as a supplement to other types of read-alouds as encouraged by Cooper (1997).

Student storytelling is motivational. It encourages students to read, and it encourages students to participate. When conducting their own research into storytelling, Doll, Benedetti, and Carmody (2001) discovered that students who didn't usually speak in class wanted to tell stories and that storytelling was a "hook" that interested reluctant readers in books.

Additionally, from my own classroom experience I've come to recognize several benefits from student-performed stories. First, students must read many stories to select one to prepare to tell. Once the student selects his or her story, she or he must read it several times which aids in developing reading fluency. Students rehearse their stories, and this leads to improved public speaking skills; and, finally, students practice active listening skills when they listen to each others' stories. Macdonald (1993, p. 43) describes her experience with storytelling in even greater detail when she says, "It [storytelling] models fine use of oral language. It models plot, sequencing, characterization, the many literacy devices you wish to convey."

Most importantly, teacher and student storytelling draws from a rich source of literature that is culturally, ethnically, and historically diverse yet universal in its description and inclusion of common human qualities. Storytelling is part of the oral tradition of many cultural groups. Therefore, every person and every culture have stories which "allow children to relate what is similar between people of various times and places" (Combs & Beach, 1994, p. 465).

Because I want my students to engage in storytelling and therefore be a part of the classroom read-aloud program, I begin the process of preparing them to tell stories by telling stories myself. I tell a different story each day as I introduce the different types of tales. (Note: I generally focus on the 10 different types of stories described later in this chapter. Please be aware that during some school years I may introduce five different types of stories first semester and five different types during second semester. Other years, depending upon the needs and interests of my students, I may focus on only four or five types of stories throughout the year. Storytelling, like all of the different types of read-alouds and performance reading routines described in this book, allows for instructional flexibility.)

The first type of story I model is the personal story. As mentioned earlier, everyone has a story to tell, and it's easier for students to talk about themselves as first-time storytellers rather than trying to work with an unknown text.

I tell my personal story and then explain how students should use the "How to Choose, Plan, and Practice Your Personal Story" handout, which appears in Figure 4.1. Students are given a few days to follow the guidelines of the handout to choose, plan, and practice their personal stories. Then on story day, students are put into groups of three, allowed to find a quiet, comfortable place to stand or sit and take turns telling their stories. (Usually my classroom is too small to accommodate the groups of three, so I use the library-media center or spread out into an adjacent classroom.)

Step 1: Choose   Student Name _____

Your Personal Story should be an episode, which is a small part of your big life! An episode is a story that has a main idea or message and has a beginning, middle, and an ending. To help you think of an interesting episode, think about the topics listed below. Try to come up with story ideas on your own! THINK!

Tell about a time you or someone you know . . .

met someone interesting	got lost	made or lost a friend
got a pet	went on vacation	were afraid
gave or received a special gift	were helpful	won something
did something for the first time	learned a lesson	were brave
were part of a special celebration	were surprised	were proud

Step 2: Plan

Now that you've decided upon a story, use the space below to select the details you would like to include and to plan the sequence of events that make up your story.

The people in my story are . . .

My story takes place . . .

The main idea or message of my story is . . .

The events that make up the beginning of my story are . . .

The events that make up the middle of my story are . . .

The events that lead to the conclusion of my story are . . .

Step 3: Practice

If you practice your story three times, you will be more confident, you'll remember your story better, and you'll enjoy your storytelling experience more. Mark each time you practice.

Practice by yourself.	Practice with two others.	Practice by yourself.
Think through your story.	Accept helpful suggestions.	Incorporate suggestions.
Don't memorize.	Learn from others stories.	Tell the story from your
	Learn by watching.	heart—not your memory.

Figure 4.1   How to Choose, Plan, and Practice Your Personal Story

After each student has had an opportunity to tell a personal story, I begin to model different types of stories. After each day's telling, I put out a book display in my classroom of the stories that fit each story category so students can read them during independent reading time. After I've modeled five different story types, the students begin to prepare for their storytellings.

I try to gather picture books and story anthologies on a library cart in my classroom. This allows students easy access to the materials and me the opportunity to answer and ask questions as students select and read stories. Before I give students access to the books, however, I conduct a mini-lesson covering the information on the first part of the Storytelling Tip Sheet in Figure 4.2 entitled "How to Select a Story That's Just Right for You." The mini-lesson is somewhat like a think-aloud in that I vocalize the things going through my head as I consider selecting a book to read.

Name _____

How to select a story that's just right for you

1. Are the characters interesting? Are there enough but not too many for you to handle?
2. Is the story length good for you? Are you better at telling long or short stories?
3. Do the characters speak with an accent or dialect that you can imitate?
4. Are there places in the story where you can use body movements and gestures?
5. Do you think the story will be fun to tell and your audience will enjoy it?

How to practice the story using seven simple steps

1. Read your story and write or draw on separate note cards the different main events.
2. Do not memorize your story word-for-word. Instead, memorize the first sentence of your story, the last sentence of your story, the sequence of events, and any special expressions or repeated sentences that occur in the story. Remember: Most tales have standard beginnings ("Once upon a time" or "A long time ago") and standard endings ("And they lived happily ever after" or "And that's how the elephant got its trunk.") Using these standard beginnings and endings will help your audience be better listeners because they will know when your story begins and ends.
3. Read your story again and practice telling it using your list or drawings.
4. If you can, tape record your story and listen to it frequently or shuffle through your note cards whenever you get a chance to fix the sequence of events in your mind.
5. Divide your story into sections and practice telling each section of the story. Add gestures, pauses, and body movement to help you remember important details.
6. After you know each section, put the sections together so the story is divided in half. Practice several times telling the first half of the story, and practice several times telling the second half of the story.
7. Now you are ready to put the two halves together and practice your story from beginning to ending.

How to connect with your audience when you tell your story

1. Before you begin speaking, make sure the audience is quiet and is looking at you. If you need a chair or any other piece of equipment or furniture, put it in place.
2. Begin your storytelling by stating the title of the story, the author (if there is one) and the country or region of origin.
3. Speak loudly. Vary your pace according to your story's need. Make use of pauses. Maintain eye contact. Use the gestures, body movements, and vocal intonations you practiced. Remember to tell the story from your heart—not your memory!
4. If you make a mistake, just keep going. We probably won't even notice!
5. When you are done with your story, wait for the audience to applaud before leaving the storytelling stage area.

Figure 4.2   Storytelling Tip Sheet

Because most of the picture books and stories are short, I usually require each student to read at least 10 stories. Students must also complete a log sheet (Figure 4.3) entry for each story. It is from this log sheet that each student will select the story he or she will tell.

Once the student has selected a story, I conference with him or her to verify the story she or he has selected, to answer any questions, to offer suggestions, to explain the information on the Storytelling Tip Sheet, and to go over the grading

---

Name_____

Directions: You are required to read at least 10 different stories and record each story in the spaces provided. Read a variety of different types of stories and try to read a variety of stories from many different countries. You are looking for a great story to tell! Make sure you like the story you choose to tell as you will be working with it for several days!

Title_____

Author_____

Country/Region or origin_____

Anthology_____Page_____

Story Type (Circle One):   Fable   Traditional Myth/Legend   Urban Legend   Chain

Trickster Tale   Pourquoi   Ghost-Scary Story   Tall Tale   Circle Story   Folk Tales

My thoughts about the story_____

_____

_____

Title_____

Author_____

Country/Region or origin_____

Anthology_____Page_____

Story Type (Circle One):   Fable   Traditional Myth/Legend   Urban Legend   Chain

Trickster Tale   Pourquoi   Ghost-Scary Story   Tall Tale   Circle Story   Folk Tales

My thoughts about the story_____

_____

_____

Figure 4.3   Storytelling Log Sheet

rubric (Figure 4.4). I set aside 15 minute blocks over the course of several days so students can find a corner or space in the classroom and practice telling their stories in groups of three. When I think the students are adequately prepared, I schedule five to seven stories each day so we have a week of storytelling. I also tell students to invite their parents to attend class the day they tell their stories, and I inform students that I will videotape their storytelling if they bring a videotape from home.

As the school year progresses, I continue to tell stories as an interesting supplement to my classroom read-aloud program. I can't agree more with Gregory Denham (1994, p. 6) when he says, "Whatever their tone or theme, stories reach

---

Name_____

Title_____

Author/Country/Region_____Type of Story_____

Rating Scale: (4) Outstanding   (3) Very Good   (2) Average   (1) Needs Improvement

Volume:	Could the audience hear you even when your story required you to whisper?	4 3 2 1
Comments: _____		
Pace and Timing:	Did you speak too rapidly? Too slowly? Did you vary your pace and timing to match the story?	4 3 2 1
Comments: _____		
Pronunciation:	Did you pronounce words correctly and did you speak clearly enough for all to understand?	4 3 2 1
Comments: _____		
Eye contact:	Did you maintain eye contact with your audience?	4 3 2 1
Comments: _____		
Familiarity of story:	Did you know your story well enough that you weren't struggling to remember?	4 3 2 1
Comments: _____		
Movement/Gestures:	Did you use effective body movement and gestures that added to your story?	4 3 2 1
Comments: _____		
Audience Connection:	Did your overall presentation get and keep the audience's attention?	4 3 2 1
Comments: _____		
Poise:	Did you maintain your composure before, during, and after telling your story.	4 3 2 1
Comments: _____		

Final Score and Letter Grade_____

Figure 4.4   Storytelling Rubic

out to listeners, reassuring them, reducing their alienation, and bringing a sense of belonging."

Story Suggestions

Some story type definitions have been adapted in part from Dailey (1994).

Fable

Fables are brief tales with animal characters. The stories teach a moral lesson. Fables are usually fairly easy to tell and are a good place for beginning storytellers.

Fables by Arnold Lobel (Harper & Row, 1980)

Twenty one-page fables appear in this Caldecott award-winning book.

Squids Will be Squids: Fresh Morals and Beastly Fables by Jon Scieszka and Lane Smith (Scholastic, 1998)

Scieszka and Smith understand middle school student humor. These outrageous "fables" are great fun after your students become familiar with Aesop's traditional versions.

Traditional Myth or Legend

Myths are bold, fantastical stories about gods and demigods. Although they often explain natural events, they are much broader in scope than pourquoi stories. A legend usually "revolves around an incident that is believed to have taken place or a person who may actually have lived" (Bauer, 1993, p. 139). Like myths, legends can take on fantastical natures with each retelling as they are passed from one generation to the next.

Favorite Greek Myths retold by Mary Pope Osborn (Scholastic, 1989)

These brief versions make Greek myths easily accessible to students.

Yonder Mountain: A Cherokee Legend retold by Robert H. Bushyhead and written by Kay Thorpe Bannon (Marshall Cavendish, 2002)

Chief Sky sends three warriors on a test to determine which one will be the new chief.

Urban Legend

Urban myths are bizarre stories that sound true but aren't. They're passed on and spread throughout the culture as being true stories that happened to "a friend of a friend" (Brunvand, 1985).

> *Spiders in the Hairdo: Modern Urban Legends* collected and retold by David Holt and Bill Mooney (August House, 1999).

You'll probably recognize some of these legends. "The Hook" and "The Babysitter" are classics. This book is also a good source for Short Pieces (see chapter 8).

> *The Vanishing Hitchhiker: American Urban Legends and their Meanings* by Jan Harold Brunvand (W.W. Norton, 1981).

Legends are briefly retold and then documented as to how they grew and spread. You may recall "The Kentucky Fried Rat."

Chain Story

Chain Stories are like a pile of dominos falling, knocking each one down in a chain-like reaction. All the story's events are related to each other yet are sequenced so that each event is the result of the one preceding it.

> *Why Mosquitoes Buzz in People's Ears* by Verna Aardema (Scholastic, 1975)

This cumulative pourquoi story is a classic with its stunning art and lively text.

> *Pirican Pic and Pirican Mor* by Hugh Lupton (Barefoot Books, 2003)

Lupton's version is a faithful retelling of the Scottish tale in which Pirican Mor goes to great lengths to try to reprimand Pirican Pic for eating all of the walnuts Pirican Mor shook from the tree. This story makes a fun Readers Theater for older students to perform for younger students.

Trickster Tale

Trickster tales can be divided into two broad categories. In one type of trickster tale, the main character tries to trick those around him but ends up being tricked in the end. In the other type of trickster tales, the main character uses his cleverness to trick an enemy in order to escape harm.

> *Tops and Bottoms* by Janet Stevens (Harcourt Brace, 1995)

Father Hare teaches lazy Bear a lesson about hard work.

Zorro the Rabbit: A Trickster Tale From West Africa by Gerald McDermott (Harcourt, 1992)

Rabbit seems to have the upper hand until he discovers the joke's on him.

Pourquoi

Pourquoi stories explain why things are the way they are. Some are serious and attempt to explain natural events while others offer humorous explanations.

Why the Sun and Moon Live in the Sky by Elphinstone Dayrell (Houghton Mifflin, 1968).

This West African tale recalls the day water came to visit and forced sun and moon off the earth and into the sky.

Armadillo Tattletale by Helen Ketteman (Scholastic, 2000)

This delightful story tells how armadillo ended up with tiny ears even though "In the bare bones beginning armadillo had long ears as tall as a jackrabbit's and as wide as a steer's horn."

Ghost/Scary Story

Ghost stories and scary stories deal with anything frightening as well as supernatural phenomena. Although many students love a good ghost story, it takes real talent to tell one well because of its demanding use of pauses and pacing. And I remind my students that "slasher" tales aren't ghostly—they're just gory.

Lucy Dove by Janice Del Negro (DK, 1998)

Art and just the right cadence of prose blend to make this a clever Celtic folktale about plucky Lucy Dove, who outsmarts the bogle in St. Andrew's churchyard.

The Legend of Sleepy Hollow by Robert Van Nutt (Picture Book Studio, 1995)

This is a good "middle school" version of Washington Irving's classic tale.

Tall Tale

Tall tales include incredible exaggerations and rely on main characters who are bigger than life. Tall tales take enormous energy to tell but are worth the effort.

Davy Crockett Saves the World by Rosalyn Schanzer (HarperCollins, 2001)

Davy Crockett battles Halley's Comet and wins.

Sally Ann Thunder Ann Whirlwind Crocket by Caron Lee Cohen (Mulberry Books, 1993)

Davy Crockett's wife Sally Ann gains fame of her own when she takes on a gang of alligators and creates The Great Alligator Tornado.

Circle Story

These delightful stories end just like they begin, but the main character learns a valuable lesson during the events that occur between the beginning and the ending. There is usually a lot of repetition in a circle story.

The Greatest of All: A Japanese Folktale by Eric Kimmel (Holiday House, 1995)

Father Mouse seeks a suitable husband for his daughter—one who is "the greatest of all."

Too Much Noise by Ann McGovern (Trumpet, 1967)

Peter gets the peace and quiet he seeks after following the village wise man's instructions.

Folk Tales

Folk tales were originally stories handed down from generation to generation. Now, however, most tales are written down and have moved from being part of the oral tradition to being part of the literary tradition. In addition, modern writers have created original tales written in the folk tale tradition. Most importantly, folk tales come from around the world and can be a rich source of multicultural literature in today's classroom.

The Faithful Friend by Robert D. San Souci (Simon & Schuster, 1995)

In this West Indian folktale, a young man is willing to risk his friend's scorn and that of his new fiancé in order to protect them.

The Girl Who Wore Too Much: A Folktale From Thailand by Margaret Read MacDonald (August House, 1998)

A cautionary tale about a girl who at first chooses clothing over kindness and accuses her friends of being jealous.

References

Bauer, C. F. (1993). *New handbook for storytellers*. Chicago: American Library Association.

Brunvand, J. (1985). Urban legends in the making: Write me if you've heard this. *Whole Earth Review*, Fall, 124–130.

Colwell, E. (1983). What is storytelling? *Horn Book, 59,* 279–286.

Combs, M., & Beach, J. (1994). Stories and storytelling: Personalizing the social studies. *The Reading Teacher, 47* (6), 464–471.

Cooper, J. D. (1997). *Literacy: Helping children construct meaning.* Boston: Houghton Mifflin.

Dailey, S. (1994). Storytelling and writing. In *Tales as Tools: The Power of Story in the Classroom* (pp. 68–70). The National Storytelling Association. Jonesborough, TN: The National Storytelling Press.

Denman, G. (1994). Daring to tell: The making of a storyteller. In *Tales as tools: The power of story in the classroom* (pp. 4–6). The National Storytelling Association. Jonesborough, TN: The National Storytelling Press.

Doll, C., Benedetti, A., & Carmody, B. (2001). Unleashing the power of teenage folklore: research to investigate the power of storytelling. *Journal of Youth Services in Libraries*, 14(4), 35–41.

Farrell, C. (1991). *Storytelling: A guide for teachers.* New York: Scholastic.

Forest, H. (2000). Musings: A story arts newsletter. Available at http://www.storyarts.org/lists/index.html. Retrieved 6/13/03.

MacDonald, M. (1993). *The story-teller's start-up book.* Little Rock, AK: August House.

Moen, C. (1992). *Better than book reports.* New York: Scholastic.

Moir, H. (1994). Echoes of stories past: Storytelling as an introduction to literature. In *Tales as tools: The power of story in the classroom* (pp. 53–59). The National Storytelling Association. Jonesborough, TN: The National Storytelling Press.

Nessel, D. D. (1985). Storytelling in the reading program. *The Reading Teacher, 38* (4), 378–381.

Searle, D. (1984). Scaffolding: Who's building whose building? *Language Arts, 64,* 480–483.

Trostle, S., & Hicks, S. (1998). The effects of storytelling versus story reading on comprehension and vocabulary knowledge of British primary school children. *Reading Improvement, 35* (3), 127–136.

Turner, T., & Oaks, T. (1997). Stories on the spot: Introducing students to impromptu storytelling. *Childhood Education, 73* (3), 154–157.

Chapter
5

Picture Book Read-Alouds:

Affective and Effective
Literacy Entry Points

As the author of *Teaching With Caldecott Books* (Scholastic 1991), I have been enamored with picture books for some time. Quality picture books like the Caldecott award-winning books are "twice-told" stories (Goodman, 1987), which are stories that students experience twice through the unique blend of words and illustrations. Julius Lester, in his acceptance speech for the Caldecott award he and Jerry Pinkney received for *John Henry* (Dial, 1994) described the same concept but much more eloquently when he said, "At its best a picture book should so join word and image that the two make a whole and become more than either could be alone."

Of course, picture books belong in elementary classrooms; and educators, for good reasons, have long championed their use in middle and secondary schools as well. First, the language used in many picture books is extremely sophisticated. Most picture books are no longer written using controlled vocabulary reading levels that often leave books sounding stilted and lifeless (Billman, 2002). Secondly, the topics of many of today's picture books address such difficult issues as war, child slavery, and urban riots. As a result, many of today's picture books are intended for more mature readers (Martinzes, Roser, & Strecker, 2000). Additionally, picture books also belong in your middle school classroom because your students may have missed being exposed to many of them as they progressed through the upper elementary grades and into middle school (Neal & Moore, 1992).

However, despite its use of a variety of mature topics and its sophisticated language, a picture book is still a picture book—and, therein, lies the beauty and the reason they belong in your middle school read-aloud program as affective and effective literacy entry points.

To begin with, picture books focus on one topic. This is a refreshing change for students who must read dense textbooks which often describe several topics on a single page. By focusing on one topic, students can become curious about a topic without being overwhelmed with information or rushed to another topic. Thus picture books are affective literacy entry points because they allow for students' curiosity, and they are effective literacy entry points because they focus on one topic and allow for information management.

Secondly, picture books appeal to today's students who are growing up in a visually oriented society. Our students' web literacies (Sorapure, Inglesby, & Yatchisin, 1998) are often quite sophisticated. This ability to "read" pictures and other nontext material to aide comprehension is a plus. At the same time, there are students who use pictures or illustrations as comprehension aides because English is their second language and/or because they are struggling readers who do not have the metacognitive ability to make pictures in their heads themselves when they read. For these readers, reading is not "hearing the page silently speak" (Farrell, 1966, p. 41). For readers who can't make the words speak to them in their minds, pictures and illustrations help the text "do the talking." Thus pictures books can serve as affective literacy points because they are visually appealing. At the same time, they are effective literacy entry points because they are illustrated texts that can help struggling readers and ELL students.

Finally, picture books allow for text-supported student discussion. Of course, other types of written material allow students the opportunity to go back to the text and use portions of it to prove or disprove a point; however, because a picture book focuses on one topic and is shorter than a novel or even most short stories, students are able to "lift text" easier during discussion. Thus picture books are affective literacy entry points because they allow for student discussion, which is a desirable middle school classroom activity. At the same time, picture books are effective literacy entry points because they allow students to practice "lifting text" to support their ideas without the time-consuming and sometimes confusing task of hunting through long passages.

In addition to providing a rationale for using picture books in the middle school classroom, I'd like to share with you the criteria I use for selecting books to share with students, a description of how to share books in the classroom setting, and routines I use when reading aloud pictures books.

With the enormous number of picture books being published each year, it's easy to be overwhelmed if you don't focus your search to find quality books quickly and conveniently. To keep up-to-date on picture books being published and to read only the ones I may consider for my classroom, I use the following resources to limit my search:

1. School and public library-media specialists
2. *The Reading Teacher* published by the International Reading Association
3. *Book Links* and *Booklist* published by the American Library Association
4. *The Bulletin of the Center for Children's Books* published by The Center for Children's Books
5. *The Hornbook Magazine*
6. Book review web sites listed at the end of this chapter

It may seem that I read a lot to avoid reading a lot, but quick scans of the book titles, descriptions, and authors in the resources I've mentioned allow me to pick the few books that I choose to read for consideration. Consequently, I've found that it takes a little time to save a lot of time later.

Once I've made the effort to get a new picture book to review, I read it keeping in mind the criteria I've established which include the following questions:

1. Is the subject matter appropriate for my students, and will it appeal to them?
2. Is the text appropriate for my students, and will it support student discussion?
3. Are the pictures and illustrations appropriate for my students, and do they add interest and information to the text?
4. Is the information in the book accurate and are facts and opinions differentiated?
5. Will this picture book help generate students' interest in a longer book on a similar topic if a longer book is offered to them?
6. Will students pick up this book after the read-aloud and read it again on their own during independent reading time?

Once I've selected a picture book to read aloud, I need to consider exactly how I'm going to do that—not pedagogically, but physically! The photographs of elementary students gathered on the floor around a teacher sitting in a chair while she or he shows the pages while reading a picture book are endearing, but they are not images possible in most middle school classrooms. Most middle school classes usually have 30 or more students, and in many middle schools carpeting is being removed from floors because of air-quality issues. So how can a middle school teacher share picture books, which come in all shapes and sizes, with his or her students? By planning ahead.

In very large classes, I have students remain in their seats while I stand to read. I hold the book open to show the illustrations and walk back and forth across the front of the classroom, pausing at times to go down each aisle a little way to show illustrations. (Years ago, I used to put each page under an opaque projector, and project the image onto a screen, but opaque projectors are difficult to find these days because of their limited use.) In smaller classes, I "stack" students into a "stadium-type" semi-circular audience by having some of the students sit in the back of the classroom on high stools taken from the classroom's Readers Theater corner. Next, I have students sit in desks. The bottom "row" of students sits on pillows on the floor in front of the high chair I use when I read. As with the larger group, I hold the book open to show the pictures and illustrations as I read and pause so students can examine pages more closely. (Note: When using picture books as read-alouds, I make sure the students who need to see the pictures and illustrations get the opportunity to do so. I make sure those students sit up front or I go down the aisle to them without making it obvious to the other students why I'm doing so.)

Because I believe picture books are affective and effective literacy entry points, I use picture books in two different ways in my read-aloud program. One way I use picture books in my read-aloud program is to make reading fun. Reading should be fun, and the picture books that I read aloud to my students are often humorous. In addition, I love to learn new things; and I believe school should be a place where we can all learn new things, so I include in my picture book collection books about topics and historical events that are little known. On the other hand, a portion of the picture books in my read-aloud program are devoted to sparking students' curiosity and "selling" them on reading longer books on similar topics, a concept referred to in Judith Irvin's (1990) book *Reading and the Middle School Student*.

Because I have two different types of picture book read-alouds, I use two different organizers to help facilitate student discussion. For picture books that I read aloud to entertain and inform, I give students the organizer that appears in Figure 5.1.

At the beginning of the school year, I model for my students the types of responses they might write or draw in each of the categories. And because I require my students to keep all of their handouts in a three-ring binder, they essentially maintain a log of our picture book read-alouds.

The other type of organizer I use is for picture books that I read aloud to spark students' curiosity or to sell them on reading longer books on similar topics. This organizer appears in Figure 5. 2. Also, because my students often ask me to recommend books for them for their independent reading, this type of picture book read-aloud helps my students develop lists of books they may wish to read at a later date. (Note: At the end of the school year, I remind students to take their lists home for summer reading suggestions.)

Student Name_____

Title_____

Author_____

Starter Questions and Thoughts (Write or draw your responses to the questions or suggestions I pose before I read the book aloud.)

Comments, Questions, Connections, and Language Lifts (As you listen or after you've finished listening, write or draw any comments you wish to make, any questions you have about the text, topic, or illustrations, any connections you can make between the book and other books, movies, life experiences you've had, and any words, sentences, or phrases you wish to use to support your ideas or bring to others attention.)

Entertainment-Information Rating

4 Fantastic! One of the best I've ever heard!

3 Really Good! I'd listen to it again and/or read it again myself.

2 OK. It was ok, but I've heard and/or read better.

1 Not for Me. This book didn't catch my interest.

Figure 5.1   Entertaining and Informing Picture Books

Title of Picture Book_____

Author_____

Starter Questions (Write or draw your responses to the questions or suggestions I pose before I read the book aloud.)

Comments, Questions, Connections, and Language Lifts (As you listen or after you've finished listening, write or draw any comments you wish to make, any questions you have about the text, topic, or illustrations, any connections you can make between the book and other books, movies, life experiences you've had, and any words, sentences, or phrases you wish to use to support your ideas or bring to others attention.)

Title of Longer Book_____

Author_____

After the picture book read-aloud and the advertisement for the longer book, I think

4 Fantastic! The longer book is one I'd like to read right away!

3 Really Good! The longer book is one I'd like to read at a later date.

2 Ok. The topic is interesting, but I'm not sure. I'd have to look over the book.

1 No. The advertised longer book is not for me.

Figure 5.2   Picture Books and Longer Book Suggestions

Read-Aloud time is valuable class time and needs to have a purpose. If the picture books you choose to read aloud meet the criteria for selection, you are able to share them with your students in your classroom setting, and you plan ahead and use organizers to help facilitate student discussion, you and your students will enjoy this rich source of read-aloud material!

Resources

Entertaining Picture Books

Red Ranger Came Calling by Berkeley Breathed (LittleBrown, 1997)

Chris Van Allsburg's *Polar Express* (Houghton Mifflin, 1985) is a wonderful book for elementary school students. When students get to middle school, however, many are apt to like the humor in Red Ranger's story.

The Happy Hocky Family by Lane Smith (Viking, 1993)

This is a hilarious parody of the Dick and Jane books. (You may have to bring in a Dick and Jane "story" so students get the humor.)

Click,Clack Moo Cows That Type by Betsy Lewin (Simon & Schuster, 2000)

Give a cow a typewriter and it's likely to go on strike against Farmer Brown.

The Web Files by Margie Palatini and Richard Egielski (Hyperion, 2001)

This is a hilarious send-up of the old *Dragnet* radio and television shows featuring Ducktective Web.

The Secret Knowledge of Grown-ups by David Wisniewski (HarperTrophy, 2001)

Infectious humor helps stretch this book's conspiracy theories to the limit as kids discover the *real* reasons they have to brush their teeth and eat their vegetables.

Math Curse by Jon Scieszka and Lane Smith (Viking, 1995)

No one does outrageous humor better than Scieszka and Lane. The narrator in this story is cursed for the day because everything he encounters turns into a math problem.

Intriguing Picture Books

Riding the Tiger by Eve Bunting (Clarion, 2001)

This is an allegorical tale about gangs, bullies, and the difference between intimidation and respect.

Wilfrid Gordon McDonald Partridge by Mem Fox (ScottForesman, 1989)

Wonderfully cadenced, this book shows young Wilfrid Gordon McDonald Partridge as he sets off to help 96 year-old Miss Nancy recapture her forgotten memories.

The Three Questions by Jon J. Muth (Scholastic, 2002)

When is the best time to do things? Who is the most important one? What is the right thing to do? The book and questions are based on Leo Tolstoy's 1903 short story.

The Seed by Isabel Pin (North South Books, 2001)

Two insect tribes prepare to go to war over a seed that falls between the two tribes in this antiwar allegory reminiscent of Jonathan Swift's *Gulliver's Travels*.

The House That Crack Built by Clark Taylor (Chronicle, 1992)

This is no nursery rhyme. The book's summary statement says it all. "Cumulative verses describe the creation, distribution, and destructive effects of crack cocaine."

Interesting Picture Books
(Based on little known true events)

Sailing Home: A Story of a Childhood at Sea by Gloria Rand (North South Books, 2001)

This book is based on the journals of the Madsens family and describes the life of a real 19th century seafaring family who lived on the *John Ena*, a four-masted cargo ship.

The Race of the Birkenbeiners by Lise Lunge-Larsen (Houghton Mifflin, 2001)

Birkenbeiners, brave Norwegian warriors, fight to protect their infant king, Prince Hakon. This story is based on an account written by Sturla Tordsson in 1264.

Call Me Ahnighito by Pam Conrad (HarperCollins, 1995)

In 1897 when Robert E. Peary's expedition recovered a huge meteorite in Greenland, Peary's four-year-old daughter named it after her nanny who was a native Greenlander named (Ah-na-HEET-o). The meteorite can still be seen today in New York City's American Museum of Natural History.

Mailing May by Michael O Tunnell (HarperCollins, 2000)

In 1914 Idaho, train tickets were expensive so the parents of five-year-old Charlotte May Pierstorff fixed 53 cents postage onto her back and "mailed" her to her granparents' home 75 miles away.

Marven of the Great North Woods by Kathryn Lasky (Harcourt, 1997)

During the 1918 influenza epidemic in Duluth, Minnesota, the author's father Marven was sent to a logging camp in the north woods where he was befriended by a burly French-Canadian lumberjack named Jean-Louis.

Picture Books That Tie to Longer Books

Picture Book:	*The Day Gogo Went to Vote* by Elinor Batezat Sisulu (Little Brown, 1996)
Longer Book:	*Journey to Jo'burg: A South African Story* by Beverley Naidoo (Harper, 2002)
Tie:	Apartheid and poverty, the 1994 elections in South Africa
Picture Book:	*Kate's Wish* by Barbara Shook Hazen (Dial, 2002)
Longer Book:	*Feed the Children First: Irish Memories of the Great Hunger* edited by Mary E. Lyons (Atheneum, 2002)
Tie:	Irish famine and emigration
Picture Book:	*The Great Serum Race: Blazing the Iditarod Trail* by Debbie Miller (Walker, 2002)
Longer Book:	*Winterdance: The Fine Madness of Running the Iditarod* by Gary Paulsen (Harvest, 1995)
Tie:	History of the Iditarod and the race as it is today
Picture Book:	*Randolph's Dream* by Judith Mellecker (Random House, 1991)
Longer Book:	*Good Night, Mr. Tom* by M. Magorian (Harper Row, 1982)
Tie:	Children evacuated from cities to the country in WW II England
Picture Book:	*Frightful's Daughter* by Jean Craighead George (Dutton, 2002)
Longer Book:	*Frightful's Mountain* by Jean Craighead George (Puffin, 2001)
Tie:	The end of the Mountain trilogy and the introduction of another peregrine, Oksi
Picture Book:	*The Bobbin Girl* by Emily Arnold McCully (Dial, 1996)
Longer Book:	*Lyddie* by Katherine Paterson (Puffin, 1994)
Tie:	The textile mills of Lowell, Massachusetts, in the 1830s
Picture Book:	*Hiroshima No Pika* by Toshi Maruki (Lothrop & Lee, 1980)
Longer Book:	*Hiroshima* by John Hersey (Vintage, 1989)
Tie:	The bombing of Hiroshima and its aftermath

Picture Book: *The Cello of Mr. O* by Jane Cutler (Dutton, 1999)
Longer Book: *My Palace of Leaves in Sarajevo* by Marybeth Lorbiecki
                   (Dial, 1997)
Tie: Children caught in war-torn countries

Picture Book: *Under the Quilt of Night* by Deborah Hopkinson (Ath-
                   eneum, 2002)
Longer Book: *North by Night: A Story of the Underground Railroad* by
                   Katherine Ayres (Yearling, 2000)
Tie: Escaping slavery on the Underground Railroad

Picture Book: *Patrol: An American Soldier in Vietnam* by Walter Dean
                   Myers (HarperCollins, 2002)
Longer Book: *Fallen Angels* by Walter Dean Myers (Bt. Bound, 1999)
Tie: American soldiers' experiences in Vietnam

Picture Book: *Train to Somewhere* by Eve Bunting (Scholastic, 1996)
Longer Book: *Rodzina* by Karen Cushman (Clarion, 2003)
Tie: Children traveling on the Orphan Trains in 1850s to late
                   1920s

Picture Book: *The Mary Celeste: An Unsolved Mystery From History* by
                   Jane Yolen and Heidi Elisabet Yolen Stemple (Scholas-
                   tic, 1999)
Longer Book: *Left for Dead: A Young Man's Search for Justice for the
                   USS Indianapolis* by Pete Nelson (Delacorte, 2002)
Tie: Ships lost at sea and the theory and truth behind each
                   story

Picture Book: *Through the Tempests Dark and Wild: A Story of Mary
                   Shelley* by Sharon Darrow (Candlewick, 2003)
Longer Book: *Frankenstein* by Mary Shelley (Penguin Classics, 1992)
Tie: Mary Shelley's inspiration for her Gothic novel

Photo-Essay Text: *The Lost Boys of Natinga: A School for Sudan's Young Refu-
                   gees* by Judy Walgren (Houghton Mifflin, 1998)
Longer Book: *Dream Freedom* by Sonia Levitin (Harcourt, 2000)
Tie: Modern-day slavery of the Dinka and Nuba tribes in
                   the Sudan

Informational Text: *Getting Away With Murder: The True Story of the Emmett
                   Till Case* by Chris Crowe (P. Fogelman, 2003)
Longer Book: *Mississippi Trial, 1955* by Chris Crowe (P. Fogelman,
                   2002)
Tie: The real-life kidnapping and murder of Emmett Till

Internet Sites

Children's Literature Web Guide http://www.acs.ucalgary.cal ~ dkbrown/
index.html

This is a one-stop-shopping site for high quality links pertaining to children's
literature.

The Bulletin of the Center for Children's Books http://edfu.lis.uiuc.edu/puboff/
bccb

This is the electronic version of this leading children's book review journal.

Nancy Polette Online http://nancypolette.com/home.htm

An easy, friendly site that describes this educator's favorite new books.

American Library Association http://www.ala.org/alsc/

Go to this site for easy access to the entire list of the Newbery, Caldecott, and
Coretta Scott King Award winning books.

References

Billman, L. W. (2002). Aren't these books for little kids? *Educational Leadership*,
   60 (3), 48–51.

Farrell, E. J. (1966). Listen, my children, and you shall read . . ." *English Journal*,
   55 (1), 39–45.

Goodman, K. S. (1987). *Language and thinking in school: A whole language curriculum.* New York: Richard C. Owen.

Irvin, J. (1990). *Reading and the middle school student.* Boston, MA: Allyn &
   Bacon.

Martinez, M., Roser, N., & Streckers, S. (2000). Using picture books with older
   students. In K. Wood & T. Dickinson (Eds.), *Promoting literacy in grades 4–9:
   A handbook for teachers and administrators* (pp. 250–262). Boston: Allyn &
   Bacon.

Moen, C. (1991). *Teaching with Caldecott books.* New York: Scholastic.

Neal, J. C. & Moore, K. (1992). The very hungry caterpillar meets Beowulf in
   secondary classrooms. *Journal of Reading, 35,* 290–296.

Sorapure, M., Inglesby, P., & Yatchisin, G. (1998). Web literacy: Challenges and
   opportunities for research in a new medium. *Computers and Composition,
   15,* 409–424.

Chapter 6

Musical Read-Alouds:

Combinations That Hit the Right Notes

Although individual tastes vary, it is indeed rare for anyone to dislike music. Even in its basic form, music surrounds us in the tapping of the keyboard, the staccato of the rain on the window, and the assonance in a T. S. Eliot poem.

Schools have been providing students with music training for decades, and a significant amount of brain research has been completed confirming the relationship and describing the impact of music training on student achievement in the areas of math (Catterall, Chapleau, & Iwanaga, 1999), reading performance (Hurwitz, Wolf, Bortnick, & Kokas, 1975), creativity (Wolff, 1979), cognition (Shaw, 2000), and verbal memories (Chan, Ho, & Cheung, 1998). However, music can be heard in many other areas in schools far from bustling chorus and band rooms. Music is being played in regular classrooms to stimulate creative writing (Scott, 1996), to expand children's shared books experiences, sight vocabulary, and comprehension (Kolb, 1996), to teach content area material (Bean, 1997) and as part of character education programs (Wellington, 2003).

Since natural and created music seem to be just about everywhere, using music to enhance and to accompany read-alouds is aesthetically and cognitively appropriate. First, it's important to acknowledge that reading aloud can be a musical event in itself. Poetry certainly can have a rhythm and tone with its combinations of words and its deft use of alliteration and assonance. Moreover, the combination of syllables in the lines of text not only in plays but also on the pages of countless picture books and YA novels can establish a cadence that can only be described as a "symphony of words."

Aside from music coming *from* the words, music can be used *with* the words as well. Two studies suggest that using background music can enhance learning performance by helping students focus their thinking (Hall, 1952; Cockerton, Moore, & Norman, 1997). In another study, the reading comprehension of 8th and 9th grade students substantially improved when background music was played (Giles, 1991). Eric Jensen (2001), in *Arts With the Brain in Mind,* recommends that background music be balanced, predictable, and be orchestral instrumentals rather than music with lyrics, which can distract students.

In addition to helping students focus, music in the classroom can evoke as well as provoke emotions (Blood, Zatorre, Bermudez, & Evans, 1999). Jensen (1998, 2001) notes that emotions create physical pathways and chemical responses in the brain, and it is also known that music can influence heart rate (Mockel et al., 1994) and blood pressure (Brownley, McMurray, & Hackney, 1995). If you have any doubt that there is a music-emotion connection, think of how music is purposefully used to enhance movies. Ordinary movies can have extraordinary scenes that are more exhilarating, more frightening, or more sorrowful due to the movie's musical score. Certainly we do not want to be Machiavellian and manipulate students' emotions. However, emotions frame and permeate all learning. As Jensen (2001, p. 80) points out, "Good learning does not avoid emotions, it embraces them."

The musical read-alouds suggested later in this chapter support the two purposes mentioned earlier. First, music can be used to help students focus their thinking; and secondly, music can be used to create an emotional "tie" to literature. However, before going into detail as to how you can achieve these purposes, let me offer some broad suggestions for finding, cataloging, and playing music in your classroom.

You can take several approaches to finding the right music to fit your needs. First, become good friends with your building's or school district's music teacher. Once she or he discovers that your purpose is to use more music in your classroom, you will have won him or her over. Next, become familiar with the music collection at your local library. You may be amazed at the extent and variety of music available to you free of charge. Also, never pass a bargain bin of CD's or cassette tapes in discount and warehouse stores. Finally, check specials at online book and music outlets. (These same outlets often let you listen to a small portion of a CD before purchasing it, and some even offer free downloads.)

Once I've found a CD or a song I want to use, I "catalog" it so I don't have to repeat my search if I want to use it year after year. For example, I'd been reading aloud Rosemary Well's *Mary on Horseback* (Puffin, 1998) every year to each group of students assigned to my classroom since the book's publication. The book's simple yet touching stories describe how Mary Breckenridge brought health care to the people living in Appalachia in the 1930s. I knew country music would be appropriate for this read-aloud, but I didn't hear anything that would actually enhance the stories until I saw the movie *O Brother Where Art Thou?* and bought the soundtrack (UMG Recordings, 2000). Now I use "I am a Man of Constant Sorrow" performed by Norman Blake. This "mountain music" creates the exact mood to help transport students not only back in time but also up into the primitive mountains.

To "catalog" this musical read-aloud, I write the title of the book and song on a note card along with a description of the story, the amount of time the read-aloud lasts, the length of the song, and any specifics about how to use the song during the read-aloud. If I don't own the book and/or music, I also record where I got each on the note card. A sample entry along with a blank one for your use appears in Figures 6.1 and 6.2.

Text Title "*How Many Stars in my Crown*"
Author *Rosemary Wells*
Found in *Mary on Horseback*
Music Title "*I am a Man of Constant Sorrow*" *Norman Blake*
Found on *O, Brother, Where Art Thou? CD*
Text Location *Classroom library*
Music Location *home collection*
Length of read-aloud and music notes: *Approx 10 min. Let music play before saying story title. Play during pgs 39-42. Read to pg. 47 w/o music. At bottom of pg 47 start music again. Play to end and beyond.*
Dates Used ___ *5/10/02* *9/20/03* ___

Figure 6.1   Musical Read-Aloud Catalog Example.

For general background music, I use "easy listening" music and generic relaxation piano and harp music. I use this type of music to help students focus during their independent reading time. Because I use these selections often and randomly, I keep my general background music CD's and cassette tapes in my classroom all of the time and rotate selections on a regular basis. Additionally, I don't catalog these materials other than to note that each CD or cassette is in its

Text Title _____

Author _____

Found in _____

Music Title _____

Found on _____

Text Location _____

Music Location _____

Length of read-aloud and music notes:

Dates Used_____ _____ _____ _____ _____

Text Title _____

Author _____

Found in _____

Music Title _____

Found on _____

Text Location _____

Music Location _____

Length of read-aloud and music notes:

Dates Used_____ _____ _____ _____ _____

Figure 6.2   Musical Read-Aloud Catalog Cards.

proper case. Consequently, I use background music to help my students focus as Jansen (2001) suggests, but my practice of using music to help students focus during read-alouds is much more song-specific than playing orchestral instrumentals.

Music selections that I use to help students focus during read-alouds are specific pieces of music that become part of the story and, therefore, part of the read-aloud. Often a musical selection is mentioned in the text. This is the case in Howard Kaplan's sad but beautiful book, *Waiting to Sing* (DK, 2000) in which Beethoven's *Fur Elise* is an integral part of the story. In other books, playing an artist's or composer's music as part of the read-alouds gives students needed background information. A case in point is when I read aloud portions of the biography of Woody Guthrie entitled *This Land Was Made for You and Me* by Elizabeth Partridge (Viking, 2002). Although the book is exquisite, students can gain an even better understanding of this dust-bowl troubadour if they not only read the book but also listen to the music he wrote and performed during his lifetime.

Music selections that I use to help create emotional "ties" to literature tend to be selections that create mood or help establish the tone of a book. During this type of musical read-aloud, I usually play a music selection prior to reading aloud the story and ask students to describe the music and predict any connections that "tie" the music to the story. A musical read-aloud of this nature is the use of "mountain music" with Rosemary Well's *Mary on Horseback* (Puffin, 1998), which I described earlier in this chapter.

Although I tend to group musical read-alouds into two categories based on the purposes of focusing students' thinking or creating emotional ties between music and literature—each category really is not separate and distinct. The categories overlap, like the aesthetic and cognitive purposes of musical read-alouds. Thus the listings of books and music that appear later in this chapter should be viewed as helpful suggestions for those who wish to begin or to continue to build a collection of musical read-alouds for their own classrooms.

Because musical read-alouds are usually something new to many of my students, I try to stimulate what I call my students' musical "vision." I give students a mixed-up list of the different titles of Modest Mussorgsky's *Pictures at an Exhibition*, explain some details about Mussorgsky and his friends Victor Hartmann and Vladimir Stasovask, and then have students listen to the composition and try to match each musical selection to its title. Once the entire piece is over, I give students the correct order of the titles. Although I've had only one student in the past five years name the titles in the correct order, many students correctly label over half of the selections. Most recently, I've been sharing with students Anna Harwell Celenza's book of *Pictures at an Exhibition* (Charlesbridge, 2003) which not only gives rich details about Modest Mussorgyky's music and Victor Hartmann's artwork but also includes an excellent piano and orchestral version of Mussorgsky's *Pictures at an Exhibition*. For younger students, I recommend Jae Soo Liu and Dong Il Sheen's wordless picture book *Yellow Umbrella* (Kane Miller, 2002) to help you stimulate your students' musical "vision." Play the CD which accompanies the book and have students draw pictures representative of the music. Once the music is done, show the book's illustrations and have students compare and contrast their drawings with the book's artwork.

Once your students become accustomed to musical read-alouds and you become proficient at blending literature and music, you and your students will put this type of read-alouds at the "top of the charts"!

Musical Read-Alouds
That Focus Students' Attention

Book: *What Charlie Heard* by Mordicai Gerstein (Farrar, Straus, & Giroux, 2002). Music surrounded Charles Ives, and he heard it coming from his father's piano, the clock on the mantel, the crack of a baseball bat. "It was all noise, and music was glorious noise." *What Charlie Heard* may be your students' first introduction to this decidedly different composer whose recognition came late in life and whose music is, well—noisy!

Music: *A Set of Pieces: Music by Charles Ives* performed by Eric Bartlett and Ronnie Bauch (Polygram Records, 1994). (Note: At the time of this writing, you could hear 30 seconds of five different selections from this CD at <u>amazon.com</u>.)

Read-Aloud
Suggestions: Begin by asking students to identify the types of music they appreciate listening to and the types of music they do not appreciate listening to. Read the book and then play a selection. Enjoy your students' reactions!

Book: *No More! Stories and Songs of Slave Resistance* by Doreen Rappaport (Candlewick, 2002). Slavery is an issue I explore with my students when we read background information about the Greeks prior to reading Greek Myths. It is an issue we discuss as we explore research topics such as child labor laws, and I read Russell Freedman's book *Kids at Work: Lewis Hine and the Crusade Against Child Labor* (Clarion, 1998); and, of course, slavery is an issue with which we come face-to-face when we read American Civil War historical fiction and nonfiction. When I discovered *No More! Stories and Songs of Slave Resistance*, I was able to put away many of the bits and pieces of other books and magazines I'd cobbled together because Rappaport does such a masterful job of writing first-person accounts of familiar historical figures and also creates first-person accounts of little known slaves from composites of real people.

Music: *Steal Away-Music of the Underground Railroad* by Kim and Reggie Harris (Appleseed Records, 1998)

Read-Aloud
Suggestions: Each song is exceptional and can be played at various times of your choosing while reading aloud the first-person accounts

in *No More!* although "Go Down Moses" and "Harriet Tubman/Steal Away" are naturally more suited to the book's account of Tubman.

Book: *This Land Was Made for You and Me: The Life and Songs of Woody Guthrie* by Elizabeth Partridge (Viking, 2002). Partridge uses photographs, song lyrics, sketches, newspaper clippings, and interviews in this enormously readable text describing Guthrie's genius as an artist and his flaws as a human being. An avowed Communist, Guthrie championed the struggle of marginalized people in a time when few rules existed to protect those who picked crops, dug dams, and cleaned up after others.

Music: *Dust Bowl Ballads* (Buddha, 1940)
           The Greatest Songs of Woody Guthrie (Vanguard, (1991)

Read-Aloud
Suggestions: Select the portions of the text you wish to share with your students. I sometimes read portions of the text and play one of Guthrie's songs such as "This Land is Your Land" during a poetry unit. At other times, driven by current events and/or newspaper accounts, I read aloud portions of the text and play such songs as "Ludlow Massacre," "Deportee (Plane Wreck at Los Gatos)," and "The 1913 Massacre."

Book: *The Farwell Symphony* by Anna Harwell Celenza (Charlesbridge, 2000) Although I'm not a big fan of "packaged" books and music products, this book and CD are an exception. The story describes how composer Joseph Hayden used his "Symphony Number 45," more commonly known as the "Farewell Symphony," to coax Prince Nicholas of Austria back to his winter estate in Eisenstadt after an over-long stay in his summer palace in Hungary.

Music: A CD of Hayden's symphony, which is comprised of four movements, accompanies the book.

Read-Aloud
Suggestions: Read the first portion of the story that details the prince's arrogance towards his musicians and the musicians' unhappiness about being kept from their families because the prince wishes to remain in his summer palace well into November. Before Hayden plays the symphony for the Prince, Hayden tells the prince that the musicians inspired the music, and he

hopes the prince will find the performance "enlightening." Stop the read-aloud and play the first movement. Ask the students to describe the mood of the music and then read aloud the portion of the story that describes the prince's reaction. With the remaining three movements of the symphony, continue this pattern of playing the music, stopping, and reading aloud the appropriate portion of the text.

Book: *Once Upon a Time in Chicago: The Story of Benny Goodman* by Jonah Winter (Hyperion, 2000). "Benny liked playing the clarinet more than he liked talking" is probably one reason this son of a poor Jewish immigrant became known as "The King of Swing." Note: A lot of different circumstances came together to bring me to include Benny Goodman in my language arts class. The first year I began teaching at my current school, I was in charge of the seventh and eighth grade dances. That same year, a delightful young lady who was a dancer had her locker right outside my classroom. Of course, while doing hall duty, I talked to her a lot and learned that she and a group of her friends had taken swing dance lessons at a community center. One thing led to another and she and her friends helped teach swing dance to the eighth grade students in the gym during homeroom. At the first dance, I brought out the swing music; and to make a long story short, it is now a "tradition" at our school that eighth graders get swing dance lessons prior to the first school dance. And what better time to introduce students to "The King of Swing" than with a musical literature read-aloud about the legendary Benny Goodman.

Music: *The Very Best of Benny Goodman* (RCA, 2000)

Read-Aloud
Suggestions: I play part of "Bugle Call Rag" after reading the book's brief biography of Goodman followed by parts of "Sweet Georgia Brown" (p. 18), "St. Louis Blues" (p. 20), and "Moonaglow" (p. 26). I end with "Sing, Sing, Sing (with a Swing)."

Musical Read-Alouds that
Create Emotional Tie to Literature

Book: *Waiting to Sing* by Howard Kaplan (DK, 2000). This beauti-
                 ful, sad, yet hopeful story is about a family whose "story was
                 played on the piano." When the mother in the story becomes
                 ill, she requests Beethoven's *Fur Elise* and her son plays it on
                 the piano for her. When the mother dies, the family becomes
                 quiet until one day the father uses music to bring the family
                 "back to life."

Music: Almost any Beethoven CD has *Fur Elise*.

Read-Aloud
Suggestions: I begin the story by giving students some background about
                 the musical selection and playing the music for a short time
                 so they become familiar with it. I then begin to read aloud the
                 story and pause the CD. I continue reading aloud and playing
                 portions of the tune where it's indicated by the text. I end the
                 read-aloud by playing *Fur Elise* again without interruption.

Book: *Grandma's Records* by Eric Velasquez (Walker & Company,
                 2001). Eric spends his summer vacations in Spanish Harlem
                 ("El Barrio") where he has a special relationship with his
                 grandmother, who loves music. The highlight of one sum-
                 mer vacation is when Grandmother and Eric attend a concert
                 performed by real-life legend Rafael Cortijo and his group.
                 At subsequent times Eric shares all kinds of music with his
                 Grandmother, and he grows up to be a radio station DJ.
                 Velasquez recreates the album cover *Cortijo y s Combo* in the
                 picture book and nicely blends several Spanish phrases into
                 the text.

Music: *Cortijo and His Times* (Musical Productions, 1974)
 Latin: *The Essential Album* (Manteca, 2001)

Read-Aloud
Suggestions: Rafael Cortijo, a famous Cuban musician of the 1950s and
                 1960s, is considered the "father" of the Bomba-Plena sound,
                 which is a blend of Spanish and African music sounds. There
                 are several different places where you can play music during

this read-aloud such as when the group is eating lunch and Eric is playing the record Cortijo has brought with him. At other times, the text indicates when you should play the songs *En mi Viejo San Juan* and *El Bombon de Elena*.

Book: *The Orphan Singer* by Emily Arnold McCully (Arthur A. Levine Books, 2001). This beautifully illustrated picture book tells the story of a poor Eighteenth Century Venetian family whose only hope to obtain musical training for their tiny daughter Nina is to give her away. The Dolcis leave Nina at the ospedalo, a type of orphanage which provided the girls with musical training. Nina, renamed Catarina, eventually becomes a great singer and a loving daughter in the Dolcis family.

Music: 25 Vivaldi Favorites (Vox, 1999) (Note: I am not a huge fan of opera, but I like Vivaldi. I chose this CD because it was very inexpensive, and I could enjoy the orchestral selections and still use tract 14 with my read-aloud, which is the only female vocal selection on the CD.)

Read-Alouds
Suggestions: Since Vivaldi was Maestro for many years at the Pieta, a famous ospedalo in Venice, I play snippets of the opening movement of Vivaldi's *Stabat Mater in F Minor* four times during the story. (I play the same song and simply pause the CD while I continue to read the story.) I play music at the following times: (1) when Catarain gives a concert and the Dolci's cluster under the ospedalo's windows; (2) when Catarina sings to Antonio, who is sick in bed; (3) when Catarian appears on stage when she is eighteen; and (4) at the end of the story when the Dolcis family is singing together.

Book: *John Coltrane's Giant Steps* by Chris Raschka (Atheneum, 2002). Chris Raschka pays tribute to John Coltrane in this delightful book in which Coltrane's musical composition *Giant Steps* is "performed" by a box, a snowflake, some raindrops and a kitten.

Music: *The Very Best of John Coltrane* (Rhino, 2000)

Read-Aloud
Suggestions: Timing has a lot to do with Coltrane's music, and blending Raschka's book to Coltrane's Giant Steps, which on this CD

last 4 minutes and 43 seconds, may take a little practice, but it's worth the effort. Before I begin the read-aloud, I tell students about Coltrane and explain the concept behind the book. I read the first few pages, and then on page 8, I begin playing the CD. The piano comes in at around 2:56 on the CD and page 12 in the book. The piano portion last for about 45 seconds, and during that time I proceed to page 20–21 in the book where the kitten yells, "Stop!" I stop the CD and read the text. I then restart the CD after I reach page 26, and the kitten yells, "Go." I finish the book and the CD. I don't believe there is one right way or any wrong way to share this book and piece of music. If you experiment, you'll find a way that does justice to both works of art and provides you and your students with a musical literacy experience.

References

Bean, T. (1997) *Rewrite: A music strategy for exploring content area concepts.* Retrieved 6/2/03. Available at http://www.readingonline.org/articles/bats/index.html.

Blood, A. J., Zatorre, R. J., Bermudez, P., & Evans, A. C. (1999). Emotional responses to pleasant and unpleasant music correlate with activity in paralimbic brain regions. *Nature Neuroscience, 2,* 382–387.

Brownley, K. A., McMurray, R. G., & Hackney, A. C. (1995). Effects of music on physiological and affective responses to graded treadmill exercise in trained and untrained runners. *International Journal of Psychophysiology, 19* (3), 193–201.

Catterall, J. S. Chapleau, R., & Iwanaga, J. (1999). Involvement in the arts and human development: General involvement and intensive involvements in music and theater arts. In E. Fiske (Ed), *Champions of change: The impact of the arts on learning* [online report]. Washington, DC: The Arts Education Partnership and the President's Committee on the Arts and the Humanities. Available at http://www.artsedge.kennedyt-center.org/champions/.

Chan, A. S., Ho, Y. C., & Cheung, M. C. (1998). Music training improves verbal memory. *Nature, 396* (607), 128.

Cockerton, T., Moore, S., & Norman, D. (1997). Cognitive test performance and background music. *Perceptual and Motor Skills, 85,* 1435–1538.

Giles, M. M. (1991). A little background music please. *Principal Magazine,* November, 41–44.

Hall, J. (1952, February). The effect of background music on the reading comprehension of 278 eighth and ninth graders. *Journal of Educational Research*, *45*, 451–458.

Hurwitz, I., P. H. Wolf, B. D. Bortnick, & K. Kokas. (1975). Nonmusical effects of the Kodaly Music Curriculum in primary grade children. *Journal of Learning Disabilities, 8* (2), 45–51.

Jansesn, E. (1998). *Teaching with the brain in mind*. Alexandria, VA: Association Supervision and Curriculum Development.

Jansen, E. (2001). *Arts with the brain in mind*. Alexandria, VA: Association for Supervision and Curriculum Development.

Kolb, G. R. (1996). Read with a beat: Developing literacy through music and song. *The Reading Teacher, 50* (1), 76–77.

Mockel, M., Rocker, L., Stork, T., Vollert, J., Dianne, O., Eichstadt, H., Muller, R., & Horchrein, H. (1994). Immediate physiological responses of healthy volunteers to different types of music: Cardiovascular, hormonal and mental changes. *European Journal of Applied Physiology, 68*, 451–459.

Scott, L. G. (1996). Writing to music. *The Reading Teacher, 50* (2), 173–174.

Shaw, G. (2000). *Keeping Mozart in mind*. San Diego, CA: Academic Press.

Wellington, E. (2003). Reading, writing, rapping. *The Philadelphia Inquirer*. Retrieved 5/07/03. Available at www.philly.com.

Wolff, K. L. (1979). The effects of general music education on the academic achievement, perceptual-motor development, creative thinking, and school attendance of first graders. *Dissertation Abstracts International, 40*, 5359A.

Chapter

7

Nonfiction:

The Function, Form, and Finesse of the Information Text Read-Aloud

I love to learn new things, whether it's historical information about a building, a new recipe for pumpkin pie, the ingredients of a homeopathic dog shampoo, or the findings discussed in a controversial literacy report. I think people, especially students, are naturally curious. One way to tap into this great reservoir of curiosity is to include nonfiction literature, or informational text as it is increasingly being called, in your read-aloud program.

One function, therefore, of using informational text in your read-aloud program is to arouse and sate students' natural curiosity. And because the topics of informational texts range from bugs to baseball and everything in between, there is a book to match every interest, curricular area, and reading level. My own experience has taught me, "Even adults learn something new from nonfiction books designed for the juvenile market" (Vardell, 1998, p. 154).

In addition to providing information in an interesting format, informational texts can be motivational. According to author Marlene Targ Brill (2002, p. 30), nonfiction literature or informational text is "real life written down." This "real life" approach to literature appeals to adolescent males whose declining literacy skills put them at risk not only of failing academically but also of not being prepared to succeed in the workplace (Reynolds, 1991). As the mother of a son who was a once-upon-a-time struggling-reluctant reader who poured over maps and magazines but who disliked reading "made up" stories, I wholeheartedly support and confirm Herz and Gallo's (1996) findings that adolescent boys are enthusiastic readers of nonfiction and informational books. Moreover, Abrahamson and Carter (1991), long-time advocates of the use of nonfiction trade books in the classroom, support the use of informational texts in the classroom to help turn reluctant readers into life-long readers. Carter and Abrahamson (1991) further attest to the popularity of nonfiction by citing in one of their studies that 50 to 85 percent of the total juvenile book circulations in school and public libraries were nonfiction. A 50 percent nonfiction preference rate was also reported by Constance Mellon (1990) in her 3-year interest study. Aware of these studies, I can't help but think that the numbers in both studies would be higher if the studies were conducted today given the fact that the nonfiction and informational texts published within the last 10 years are far superior to the ones that were on library shelves during the years when the studies were being conducted. It appears that students who prefer informational texts are reading them aesthetically even though the text is written primarily to inform. That students can and will become readers if they are allowed and encouraged to read nonfiction and informational books is exciting news and provides a substantial reason for including informational text in your read-aloud program.

In addition to piquing students' interest and being motivational, informational texts are relevant to the academic and workplace world. Although I am not one to "teach to the test," I am aware that 50 to 85 percent of standardized tests are now comprised of informational texts (Calkins, Montgomery, Santman, & Falk, 1998). Thus it is our responsibility as educators to acquaint our students with informational texts. Moreover, beyond standardized tests, we teachers must prepare our students for the real world; and in the real world, research reveals that 86 percent of the texts read by adults are classified as informational in nature (Duke, 199,9 and Parkes, 2000, as cited by Hoyt, 2002). Including informational texts in your read-aloud program, therefore, is a sound practice that can help students meet academic and workplace demands.

Consequently, if informational texts tap into students' natural curiosity, are the type of text they often choose to read on their own, are shown to motivate reluctant readers, and are the type of text found not only on standardized tests but mainly in "real world" reading, why don't more teachers use informational texts in their read-aloud programs? While I don't want to dwell on the negative, perhaps you'll find yourself like I did, in the list of reasons that follow. Hopefully, you will find good reasons to overcome your reluctance to include informational texts in your read-aloud program.

First, read-aloud time is supposed to be an enjoyable time; and to most teachers, enjoyment reading resides in fiction or narrative texts while informational texts are kept for the times when students need to read for information. In other words, "fiction is for read-aloud time, and nonfiction is for research time" (Vardell, 1998, p. 153). I admit to having at one time the fiction for read-aloud, nonfiction for research bias; but I've discovered that by reading nonfiction aloud, I am able to "hook" my listeners with interesting information. At the same time, I'm often able to reinforce a reading skill or demonstrate a research skill, or introduce a new vocabulary word within the context of a brief nonfiction read-aloud. Another reason teachers may be reluctant to include informational texts as read-alouds is because we are not as familiar with it as we are works of fiction. I work hard to keep current with all kinds of books that may appeal to my students; and just as I read the Caldecott and Newbery winning books, I now routinely seek out the books that receive the Orbis Pictus Award given by the National Council of Teachers of English.

Cost is another factor, and I don't have an easy answer for this obstacle. Because informational texts often include photographs and lots of color and graphics, they cost more to publish than books with only text. I buy books when I can, and I borrow multiple copies from different libraries in my area. Finally, I think teachers are reluctant to use informational texts in read-alouds because they are not quite familiar with the various types or "forms" of informational texts; and they don't know quite what to do with them or, in other words, how to "finesse" their way through an informational text read-aloud.

Before getting into the details of "form" and "finesse," it's important to establish a criteria for deciding which books to include in your informational text read-aloud program. With so many books and so little time, each book needs to be a worthy component of your overall educational plan.

Before I considered new books for inclusion in my read-aloud program, I conducted a very informal interest survey with a group of 23 seventh grade students whom I had taught and whom I knew would be scheduled into my eighth grade language arts class for the following year. I explained to the students that the purpose of the "book survey" activity was to determine which topics and types of nonfiction books they would be interested in reading themselves or having read to them. Each student started with a different book, and we began the "book survey" by first agreeing on the things the students would use to judge whether to give each book a rating of *Yes* or *No*. We decided that topic, layout and use of photographs and graphics, and writing style/vocabulary would be the most important factors in deciding whether to give a book a thumbs up or a thumbs down. The students were given one minute to look at the cover of the book and consider the topic, page through the book and look at the photographs and graphics, and read the first page of the book. After one minute, the student marked *Yes* or *No* next to the title on the survey sheet and passed the book to the next student and the process began again until each student had looked at 23 different books. By no means was this book survey scientific; however, it did give me a quick snapshot of some of the topics and types of books to use with this group of students the following year. You could easily do a similar survey of your own students to determine their interests. (My results? This group of students wanted to read about people living in various parts of the world, about bizarre happenings and unusual events, and about World War II. They also liked books with authentic photographs and samples of original documents as well as a "nontextbook" writing style.)

Once I get a general idea of the topics my students and I want to read about, I judge whether to include a text in my program by using a loose combination of criteria created by Bamford and Kristo (1998) and Moss (1995) along with the types of student activities I want to use with my own informational text read-alouds.

Criteria for Selecting Informational Text for Your Read-Alouds

1. Is this book about a topic that will excite and interest my students?

2. Is this book well-written so it will hold students' attention during the read-aloud?

3. Is this book accurate, up-to-date, and free of bias?

   An important caveat is necessary because of the debate surrounding the use of "incidental fiction" in narrative-style nonfiction books. These books, dubbed "blended books" by author Gloira Skurzynski (1992), weave facts into fiction stories that often have invented characters and situations. The Magic School Bus series by Joanna Cole and Bruce Degen is an example of blended books. On the other hand, books such as *Mercedes and the Chocolate Pilot* by Margot Theis Raven (Sleeping Bear Press, 2002) are "informational picture books" that are true stories told using a narrative picture book format. Finally, at least in my mind, there are authors like Jim Murphy and Russell Freedman whose eloquent writing style and impeccable research represent the epitome of nonfiction or informational text. Consequently, I always make sure I read how the author researched his or her topic, if the author is affiliated with any special interest groups or causes, and whom the author acknowledges as sources for his or her information.

4. Will this book lend itself to one of the following read-alouds I've created?

   a   Cover-to-Cover Read, Respond and Connect

   b. Picture Walk and Talk

   c. AlphaFacts

    d. Succinct Sentences

    e. Vocabulary Appositives

5. Will this book help students become familiar with a type or "form" of informational text so students can recognize this type of text during their independent reading?

Characteristics of Text Patterns

When I'm considering an informational text for my read-aloud program, I use the above criteria; but once I select a book, I like to categorize it depending upon the book's type or form. Informational texts can be divided into an incredible number of categories including concept books, photographic essays, survey books, informational picture storybooks, and activity books, not to mention newspapers, magazines, and catalogues. However, I like to use the term "form" to categorize the structural patterns of the informational texts I use in my own classroom, so I can keep track of the various types or forms of nonfiction I introduce and reinforce with my students. I tend to use a combination of Meyer's (1975) and Hayes' (1989) classifications that include the patterns of cause-effect, comparison-contrast, problem-solution, chronological, and enumeration. I want my students to develop an overall mental "template" of these types of text patterns, but I also want to make sure students understand that these types or forms are often used in combination (Raphael & Hiebert, 1996). In other words, I emphasize that "nonfiction is often written using a combination of several organizational structures, [but] an author may select a particular organizational structure or pattern for framing the overall book" (Bamford & Kristo, 1998, p. 28). Thus the "overall framework or form" is what I want my students to recognize and be able to utilize during their independent reading to help them read strategically.

To help students become familiar with the various types or forms of text structure, I share a book or portion of a book that is very representative of each text structure. In addition, I provide students with an information sheet that explains the characteristics of each text pattern. Then when I use a book during read-aloud, I identify its text pattern or form and remind students of the characteristics and key words associated with the text pattern. For example, before reading selected excerpts of Raymond Bial's (2002) *Tenement: Immigrant Life on the Lower East Side,* I tell students that the book is an example of the enumerative text pattern because the topic of life in a tenement is broken into several subtopics so the reader can understand what it was like living in a New York tenement in the 1800s and early 1900s. I then explain the activity the students will complete during the read-aloud and establish the connection between the text pattern and the read-aloud activity. (In the case of *Tenement,* I reinforce the enumeration text pattern by reading aloud specific excerpts that explain main ideas and that contain vocabulary words so students can complete the Vocabulary Appositive activity.) The characteristics of each of these text patterns are discussed below.

- Chronological

    Characteristics: The text describes how people, places, and events change or occur over time. Look and listen for words such as *first, second, next, long ago, now,* and *finally*. An excellent example of this type of text pattern is *Model T: How Henry Ford Built a Legend* by David Weitzman (Crown Publishers, 2002)

- Compare and Contrast

    Characteristics: The text describes how facts, concepts, events, people, places, and objects are alike (compare) and different (contrast). Look and listen for words such as *however, on the other hand, compared to,* and *similarly*. An excellent example of this type of text pattern is Patricia Mckissack's *Christmas in the Big House, Christmas in the Quarters* (Scholastic, 1994).

- Cause and Effect

    Characteristics: The text describes the cause and effect relationships between events, people, places, and concepts. Look and listen for such words as *because, consequently, as a result,* and *therefore*. An excellent example of this type of text pattern is *Black Potatoes: The Story of the Great Irish Famine, 1845–1850* by Susan Campbell Bartoletti (Houghton Mifflin, 2001).

- Problem/Solution

    Characteristics: The text describes a problem and offers solutions to the problem. Look and listen for such words as *because, thus, so that,* and *therefore*. An excellent example of this type of text pattern is *Project Puffin: How We Brought Puffins Back to Egg Rock* by Stephen W. Kress as told to Pete Salmansohn (Tilbury House, 1997). (Note: I make students aware that Kress is an Audubon scientist and this is an Audubon Society book; however, because the book is factual and well-balanced, I feel comfortable using this book in class.)

- Enumeration

    Characteristics: The text uses lists and descriptive paragraphs or chapters to describe the many subtopics of the main topic. Look and listen for such words as *to begin with, for example, next,* and *for instance*. An excellent example of this type of text pattern is *Shoes* by Margery G. Nichelason (Carolrhoda Books, 1997).

Getting students to key in on the various forms or text structures takes six read-alouds. Once I'm finished introducing the different text patterns, I refer to the handout and the specific type of text pattern before each informational text read-aloud.

Student Response Activities

The last component of the informational text read-aloud is what I call the "finesse" because, if the student activity portion of the read-aloud is not handled skillfully, an informational text read-aloud can easily slip into sounding like dull, oral textbook reading. Although I always solicit background knowledge about a topic before an informational text read-aloud, I use five different student activities during and after the read-aloud depending upon the text. These activities are Cover-to-Cover Read, Respond, and Connect; Picture Walk and Talk; AlphaFacts; Succinct Sentences; and Vocabulary Appositives. The following discussion describes each of these activities and lists resources appropriate for the activity.

Cover-to-Cover Read, Respond, and Connect

As the name implies, the Cover-to-Cover Read, Respond, and Connect activity, which appears in Figure 7.1, is designed for those times I read aloud a book

Name _____

Title _____

Author _____

Explain how the cover art related to the information in the story.

This book will be available during independent reading time. Identify the portion of the text you would reread during this time and explain why you'd reread it.

Describe any personal connection you can make with this text. This connection can be in any form, e.g., a person, movie, television show, story, poem, photograph, etc.

Figure 7.1   Cover-to-Cover Read, Respond, and Connect

cover-to-cover and ask students to respond to it by making connections. For this type of read-aloud, I use information picture books whose topics and/or people my students are not familiar with. These informational picture books hold my students' attention and can easily be read cover-to-cover in one read-aloud session.

Mercedes and the Chocolate Pilot: A True Story of the Berlin Airlift and the Candy That Dropped From the Sky by Margot Theis Raven (Sleeping Bear Press, 2002). Lt. Colonel Gail S. Halvorsen, the "Chocolate Pilot" and his squadron dropped more than 20 tons of chocolate and gum during the Berlin Airlift that lasted from June 26, 1948, to September 30, 1949. On the ground among the 100,000 children in Berlin awaiting the tiny parachutes of candy was seven-year-old Mercedes Simon. This engaging story describes the impact of the candy drops, how Mercedes and Lt. Halvorsen corresponded, and how they finally met in person in 1972.

Boss of the Plains: The Hat That Won the West by Laurie Carlson (DK, 1998). This informational picture book has invented dialogue that does not detract from its authenticity. Author Laurie Carlson tells how John Batterson Stetson went from making hats in his family's hat shop in Orange, New Jersey, to making a hat that kept the sun out of a person's eyes, the rain off his back, and was sturdy enough to clean by simply knocking the dust and dirt right off of it. In a true test of fashion and function staying power, Carlson notes that Stetson's Boss of the Plains hat is still made today in Missouri.

The Librarian Who Measured the Earth by Kathryn Lasky (Little Brown, 1994). Lasky's thoughtful author's note at the beginning of the book explains how she conducted her research on Eratosthenes, a Greek who calculated the circumference of the earth over 2,000 years ago and was only in error by 200 miles. Because little is known about Eratosthenes, Lasky explains how she pieced together information for this highly readable informational picture book.

AlphaFacts

I designed AlphaFacts, which appears in Figure 7.2, after seeing Linda Hoyt's (2002) Alphaboxes. I usually use the AlphaFacts graphic organizer with information texts that have an enumeration text pattern. Because the enumeration text pattern focuses on one topic supported by many examples and details, using AlphaFacts helps student listeners decide what they think is important and record interesting facts. For example, while reading Margery Nichelason's *Shoes* (Carolrhoda, 1997), students may choose to fill AlphaFact spaces with such interesting facts as "Greek warriors wore a sandal on their left foot so they could kick their enemies" in the *L* space or "Shoes with rubber soles let kids walk silently, and this led to shoes being called 'sneakers.'" in the *S* space. (Note: Don't expect students to write neat sentences in the boxes like these example sentences. Instead, students will use abbreviations and short-hand that they can understand. Consequently, in the *L* space, you might find: 1 sandal, L. foot to kick-Grk soldier. On the other hand, some students may find it easier to draw their idea in the spaces.

Name_____

You will use this organizer for two different read-alouds. Use pen to record your facts for one read-aloud and pencil (or another color ink) for your second read-aloud.

Title_____Author_____

Title_____Author_____

a	b	c	d	e	f
g	h	i	j	k	l
m	n	o	p	q	r
s	t	u	v	w	xyz

Figure 7.2   AlphaFacts *(student examples on following 2 pages)*

Also, because I often do not read these selected informational texts cover-to-cover, I use one AlphaFacts organizer for two different books. With the first text, the student records in pen and with the second text, the student records in another color of ink or in pencil in unused spaces so the facts from each book can be distinguished from each other.

Shoes by Margery G. Nichelason (Carolrhoda, 1997). This fascinating book packs a lot of information into its 48 pages as it describes different footwear across time and across different cultures.

The Cod's Tale by Mark Kurlansky (Putnam, 2001). This entertaining book describes the impact the lowly cod has had on history and human civilization. It has lively writing, time lines, recipes, and fun facts.

The Great Fire by Jim Murphy (Scholastic, 1995). It's difficult to imagine a city like Chicago on fire, but Murphy's readable text and excellent use of photographs, maps, and original documents makes this historical event all too real.

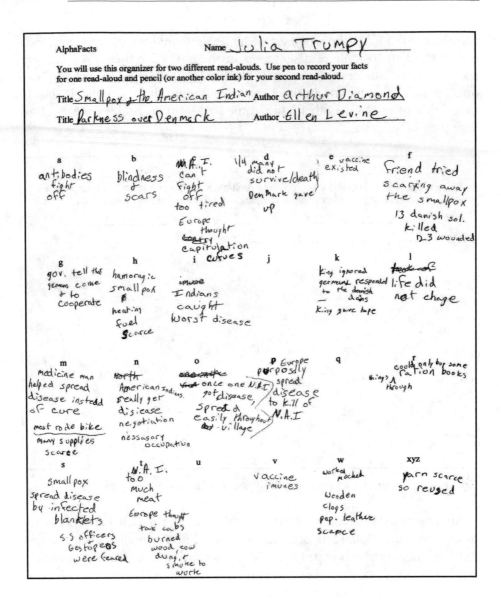

AlphaFacts   Name **Julia Trumpy**

You will use this organizer for two different read-alouds. Use pen to record your facts
for one read-aloud and pencil (or another color ink) for your second read-aloud.

Title **Smallpox & the American Indian** Author **Arthur Diamond**

Title **Darkness over Denmark** Author **Ellen Levine**

a
antibodies
fight
off

b
blindness
&
scars

c
N.A.I.
can't
fight
off
too tired

Europe
thought
~~contry~~
capitulation

d
1/4 many
did not
survive/death

Denmark gave
up

e
vaccine
existed

f
Friend tried
scaring away
the smallpox

13 danish sol.
killed
12-3 wounded

g
gov. tell the
germans come
& to
cooperate

h
hamoragic
small pox
&
heating
fuel
scarce

i cures
~~impure~~
Indians
caught
worst disease

j

k
king ignored
germans responded
to the danish
— dans
king gave hope

l
~~took of~~
life did
not chage

m
medicine man
helped spread
disease instead
of cure
~~most rode bike~~
many supplies
scarce

n
~~North~~
American Indians.
really get
disease
negotiation
nessasary
occupation

o
~~obectue~~
once one N.A.I.
got disease,
spread
easily throughout
~~but~~ village

p Europe
purposdly
spread
disease
to kill of
N.A.I

q

r
could only buy some
ration books
things through

s
Small pox
spread disease
by infected
blankets
S.S officers
&
Gestapeos
were feared

t
N.A.I.
too
much
meat
Europe thought
taxi cabs
burned
wood, cow
dung, &
smoke to
work

u

v
vaccine
imunes

w
worked mochet
Wooden
clogs
pop. leather
scarce

xyz
yarn scarce
so reused

AlphaFacts   Name Lisa LaBudde

You will use this organizer for two different read-alouds. Use pen to record your facts
for one read-aloud and pencil (or another color ink) for your second read-aloud.

Title Smallpox and the American India Author Arthur Diamond

Title Darkness over-Denmark   Author Ellen Levine

a
antibodies
to fight
off a disease
anti German

b
buffalo hides
aren't as good
as houses - theory
by breakfast country
was no longer a free nation

c
comfort for
Dans when
the king
rode

d
Danish airforce
was destroyed
before a plane
could take off

e

f
feal other tuges

g
government
has acted
like they
protected our
country from a
worse fate

h
remoragic
small pox
Hitler was always
guarded but King
Christian wasn't.

i
immune
to a disease
impossible to
live in Denmark
and not see
German soldiers

j
journalists
were permitted
to drive cars

k
King
Christian
rode through
the streets
ignored soldiers
but greeted Dans

l
living close
together spreads it
very easily

m
most American
Indians had never
faced small pox before

n

o ✓
one in four
people
died of small
pox

p
Poni were
deliberately given
the disease
~~Green police~~
Green police

q

r

s
suffered
from blindness
S.S. wore black
and skull symbols
that mean Nazi.

t

u

v
virus you
get it from
other people

w
worst type of small
pox is
variola major
wear mact
usually polite

xyz

Picture Walk and Talk

Young children often "picture walk" through a book, relying on the pictures to tell the story. The Picture Walk and Talk activity for middle school students is based on the same idea but includes an organizer to facilitate discussion. Information texts that are appropriate for the Picture Walk and Talk student activity are books in which information about the topic is conveyed primarily through the use of photographs, and these photographs are so engaging that they practically mesmerize the reader. In other words, these types of read-aloud books allow for picture/photograph examination and discussion. The Picture Walk and Talk is especially appealing to students who are visual learners.

Because the emphasis is on the photographs and graphics during this read-aloud, I try to have multiple copies of the text so students can gather in small groups to see the photographs more closely and to share their thoughts with their classmates. Because I try to have multiple copies and thus need to purchase books, I choose books that are relevant and accurate despite their older copyright dates.

When I plan this type of read-aloud, I give each student a Picture Walk and Talk graphic organizer (Figure 7.3), divide students into groups, and give each

Name _____

Title _____

Author _____

Directions: Of the eight to ten photographs-images presented during today's read-aloud, choose five to identify and to write "talking points" about. Your talking points should be in the form of observations, questions, additional information, or personal connections.

Image One   Talking Points
_____
_____
_____

Image Two   Talking Points
_____
_____

Image Three   Talking Points
_____
_____

Image Four   Talking Points
_____
_____

Image Five   Talking Points
_____
_____

Figure 7.3   Picture Walk and Talk

group a copy of the book. Students follow along to look at the images I select to point out and complete their graphic organizers. Students talk within their initial groups first and then are regrouped at random for a second discussion opportunity. Students give their final comments during an all-class wrap-up, and the books are put on display for students who wish to read more in-depth or look at more images than the ones addressed during the read-aloud.

Seeing Earth From Space by Patricia Lauber (Orchard, 1990). Despite its 1990 publication date, the photographs in this book remain stunning. They were taken from space and are grouped into categories. One category of photographs includes "sights" such as the sand dunes of the Namib Desert, Lake Natron in Tanzania, and the eye of Typhoon Pat over the Pacific Ocean. Other images are shown using remote sensing and include a Landsat image of the San Joaquin Valley in California with its cotton and wheat fields, an irrigated farmland in Saudi Arabia, and the images of ancient river beds in the Sahara Desert.

Kids at Work: Lewis Hine and the Crusade Against Child Labor by Russell Freedman (Clarion, 1994). Sixty-one of Lewis Hine's haunting photographs speak volumes as they document the drudgery and danger faced by child laborers in the United States in the early 1900s.

Fire in Their Eyes: Wildfires and the People Who Fight Them by Karen Magnuson Beil (Harcourt Brace, 1999). The photographs in this book burst off the page as they add to the text which describes the excitement and danger of the men and women who fight fires.

Succinct Sentences

I use Succinct Sentences with read-alouds and with students' independent reading to check comprehension. Almost any informational text that is divided into chapters containing well-written paragraphs is appropriate for the Succinct Sentences student activity, which appears in Figure 7.4. Although numerous books are appropriate, I try to select a chapter or specific section from a book that will entice students to pick up the book and continue reading during independent reading time.

As the title implies, students summarize a portion of the read-aloud using one or two succinct sentences. Here is a sample of what a student may write for chapter 3 "Buried Soldiers" from *The Emperor's Silent Army* by Jane O'Connor (Viking, 2002) which describes the ongoing excavation of an army of life-size terracotta soldiers and horses near Xian, China.

Succinct Sentence 1: The terracotta soldiers face east in attack position, and none of them wear helmets or carry shields.

Succinct Sentence 2: The soldiers are in a battle formation called the sword made up of archers, chariots, foot soldiers, and rear guards.

Succinct Sentence 3: In Pit 2 there are 450 terracotta Mongolian horses, chariots, and cavalrymen.

Succinct Sentence 4: Pit 3 has warriors who are talking together. Was this the army's headquarters?

Succinct Sentence 5: Long ago, wooden or clay figures were buried with dead rulers because the Chinese believed the figures would come back to life to protect the ruler's remains.

As students practice writing Succinct Sentences, they not only become more adept at discerning the overall message of the text but they also become more adept at choosing the most important details to include in their summary sentences.

Name _____

Title _____

Author _____

Directions: Listen carefully to each portion of the text as it is read aloud. When it is time to write, quickly write the most important ideas in the Notes section. When the read-aloud is completely done, go back and use the information from your Notes section to write a Succinct Sentence that summarizes the main idea for each section of text.

Notes: _____
_____

Succinct Sentence 1: _____
_____

Notes: _____
_____

Succinct Sentence 2: _____
_____

Notes: _____
_____

Succinct Sentence 3: _____
_____

Notes: _____
_____

Succinct Sentence 4: _____
_____

Notes: _____
_____

Succinct Sentence 5: _____
_____

Figure 7.4   Succinct Sentences

Black Potatoes: The Story of the Great Irish Famine, 1845–1850 by Susan Campbell Bartoletti (Houghton Mifflin, 2001). Well-researched, this book describes the human cost of the blight that destroyed the staple food of the Irish people and led to over a million deaths and the exodus of over two million Irish from their homeland.

The Good Fight: How World War II Was Won by Stephen E. Ambrose (Atheneum, 2001). Incredible photographs, readable text, and boxes of "quick facts" tell the story of WW II as it is broken into manageable topics such as "Operation Torch" and "The Invasion of Saipan."

Pick & Shovel Poet: The Journeys of Pascal D'Angelo by Jim Murphy (Clarion, 2000). Murphy captures the determination of Pascal D'Angelo, who came to this country with little and who taught himself to read and write, and weaves his story into the stories of other hardworking but hopeful immigrants of the same period.

Vocabulary Appositives

An appositive, a phrase that renames or defines a word, often appears directly after the word it renames or defines and is set off with commas. In the Vocabulary Appositives activity, which appears in Figure 7.5, students create appositive definitions for selected vocabulary words and create a visual image—that is a visual appositive to represent the vocabulary word.

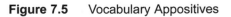

| Name |
| Title |
| Author |

Vocabulary Word	Vocabulary Appositive	Visual Appositive

Figure 7.5   Vocabulary Appositives

I select a book for this student activity if the book contains vocabulary that will help enhance my students' reading abilities and if I am able to select excerpts that use the specific vocabulary words in several meaningful ways. For example, Raymond Bial's *Tenement: Immigrant Life on the Lower East Side* (Houghton Mifflin, 2002) explains through photographs and text the terms *tenement, destitute, immigrant, regulations,* and *demolish.* At the same time, Kathryn Lasky's book *Surtsey: The Newest Place on Earth* (Hyperion, 1992) is an excellent book to introduce or reinforce such words as *eruption, intervals,* and *tumultuous,* as well as scientific words such as *fissure, lava,* and *craters.*

In the Days of the Vaqueros: America's First True Cowboys by Russell Freedman (Clarion, 2001). *Vaqueros* means cowherders and comes from the Spanish word *vaca,* which means cow. This readable text describes the historical significance of these Native Americans who taught cowboys how to be cowboys.

The Bug Scientists by Donna M. Jackson (Houghton Mifflin, 2002). This wonderfully written book describes the work of three "bug scientists," a university professor who hosts an annual Cricket Spitting Contest, a forensic entomologist who uses bugs to help solve crimes, and a myrmecologist, which is a scientist who studies ants. Dispersed throughout the book are interesting "bug bits" and an excellent glossary entitled "buzz words."

Through My Eyes by Ruby Bridges (Scholastic, 1999). Ruby Bridges describes in her own words what it was like to be six years old and the first African-American child to integrate the public schools in New Orleans in 1960.

References

Abrahamson, R. F., & Carter, B. (1991). Nonfiction: The missing piece in the middle. *English Journal, 80* (1), 52–58.

Bamford, R. A., & Kristo, J. V. (1998). Choosing quality nonfiction literature: Examining aspects of accuracy and organization. In R. A. Bamford & J. V. Kristo (Eds.), *Making facts come alive: Choosing quality nonfiction literature K–8* (pp. 19–38). Norwood, MA: Christopher-Gordon.

Brill, M. T. (2002). Nonfiction: The fun of fiction with facts. *Illinois Reading Council Journal, 30* (1), 30–35.

Calkins, L. M., Montgomery, K., Santman, D., & Falk, B. (1998). *A Teacher's guide to standardized reading tests.* Portsmouth, NH: Heinemann.

Carter, B., & Abrahamson, R. (1991). Nonfiction in a read-aloud program. *Journal of Reading, 34* (8), 638–642.

IIayes, D. (1989). Expository text structure and student learning. *Reading Horizons, 30,* 52–61.

Herz, S., & Gallo, D. (1996). *From Hinton to Hamlet: Building bridges between young adult literature and the classics.* Westport, CT: Greenwood Press.

Hoyt, L. (2002). *Make it real: Strategies for success with informational texts.* Portsmouth, NH: Heinemann.

Mellon, C. A. (1990). Leisure reading choices of rural teens. *School Library Media Quarterly, 18,* 223–228.

Meyer, B. J. F. (1975). *The organization of prose and its effect on memory.* Amsterdam: North Holland.

Moss, B. (1995). Using children's nonfiction tradebooks as read-alouds. *Language Arts, 72,* 122–126.

Raphael, T. E., & Hiebert, E. H. (1996). *Creating an integrated approach to literacy instruction.* Orlando, FL: Harcourt Brace.

Reynolds, A. J. (1991). Note on adolescents' time-use and scientific literacy. *Psychological Reports, 68,* 63–70.

Skurzynski, G. (1992). Up for discussion: Blended books. *School Library Journal, 38* (10), 46–47.

Vardell, S. M. (1998). Using read-aloud to explore the layers of nonfiction. In R. A. Bamford & J. V. Kristo (Eds.), *Making facts come alive: Choosing quality nonfiction literature K–8* (pp. 151–167). Norwood, MA: Christopher-Gordon.

Chapter 8

Novels, Short Stories, and Short Pieces:

The Long, the Short, and the Very Short Read-Aloud

Novels

When I give presentations at conferences or conduct workshops, teachers often ask me how many books I read aloud in a year. The truth is, I don't often read aloud novels to my students. In fact, I usually read only thee to five short novels each year. This takes many teachers aback since most teachers associate reading aloud with reading aloud novels.

There are two reasons I don't read aloud a lot of novels in my classroom. One reason has to do with absenteeism. Although the students who attend the school in which I teach have fairly good attendance, I find that by the end of my reading a long novel, about a fourth of the students have not heard the entire book, cover-to-cover, due to illnesses, music lessons, vision tests, dentist appointments, and all the other things that interrupt middle school students' school schedules. Frankly, instruction time is too precious to end up having several of my students getting only part of what is happening in the classroom. Another reason I don't read aloud a lot of novels is because independent reading is at the heart of my literacy program, although I do use a few "core" novels that everyone reads. Because I work hard to promote independent reading, I tend to use a "read-and-tease" Readers Theater approach with many novels to encourage students to read them on their own.

The novels that I select to read aloud are usually books that fall into one of three different categories. They are about topics that are controversial, and I want to make sure students have a forum for discussion; they are books that are so poetic that an adult oral reading is my stubborn way of making sure the students "get it"; or they are very short novels that support a core book or themed unit of materials the entire class is reading. Having given my criteria for novels I read aloud, let me add that I try to read aloud at least one humorous novel. Novels such as Carl Hiaasen's *Hoot* (Knopf, 2002), Louis Sachar's *Holes* (Farrar, Straus, & Giroux, 1998), Andrew Clements' *Frindle* (Bt. Bound, 1999), and Richard Peck's *A Long Way From Chicago* (Puffin, 2000) are perfect for those times when you and your students need to relax and enjoy a good book.

An example of a controversial book that I read aloud is Terry Trueman's *Stuck in Neutral* (HarperCollins, 2000). This riveting and sometimes disturbing novel is a story about fourteen-year old Shawn McDaniel who has cerebral palsy. He is unable to control his bodily functions and, from the outside looking in, he appears to be in pain and unable to participate in any meaningful life activity. However, Shawn is actually very happy to be alive and is a "secret genius" because he remembers everything he has ever seen or heard. Shawn learns that his father, who loves him deeply, plans to kill him in a mistaken belief that he will be ending Shawn's pain. This Michael L. Printz-award winning book keeps my students on the edge of their seats and at the end of the novel, I always leave extra time for students' comments and all-and-all "outpourings."

Often students will order *Stuck in Neutral* through a book club or ask to borrow it from me after the read-aloud is done because they want to read the parts that I skipped and/or they want to read and think about the story and the topic some more. (Note: I do not read every word in this book. I don't believe in censorship, but I do believe in being sensible. In my mind, I can't very well ask my students to use appropriate language in my classroom if I read "real-life" but *classroom inappropriate* language during our class read-aloud. I explain to my students that I edit the text just like feature films are edited for television viewing, and they understand the comparison and my reasoning.)

An example of a book that I read aloud because I want the students to "get it" is Jerry Spinelli's *Loser* (Joanna Cotler, 2002). This is a book about Donald Zinkoff, who is joyful, kind, and filled with the love of life, but who, nevertheless, is labeled a loser because of his uncontrollable giggling, sloppy handwriting, and hopeless athleticism. *Loser* is not a gripping novel, but it can grab my students if they see themselves in the pages. And because it speaks to the issue of bullying, the book's message is timely and timeless. Also, because my students read Spinelli's *Crash* (Knopf, 1996), we often wonder if Donald is the early-childhood version of Penn Webb, a kind, happy boy who is also bullied in school.

An example of a novel that I read aloud to support a themed unit is Gary Paulsen's *Nightjohn* (Laurel Leaf, 1995). This is a book about a courageous, determined man who risks his freedom to teach slaves how to read and write. Some years my students read Irene Hunt's *Across Five Aprils* (Berkley, 1987), while other years, my students read a collection of fiction and nonfiction pieces about the Civil War-era. Regardless of whether the students read the novel or the collection, I always read *Nightjohn* aloud to them.

Being aware that reading entire novels aloud is motivational to reluctant readers (Beers, 1998), each year I rethink my reasons for reading aloud only a few choice novels, and each year I go with what I know works in my classroom: I read aloud or I have a student-presented performance reading every day. Every day my students participate in or are active learners in read-alouds that include Readers Theater, Performance Poetry, Picture Books, Storytelling, Musical Literature, Informational Texts, Short Stories, Short Pieces, or a novel. By using these varied read-aloud routines, I know my reluctant readers as well as my motivated readers are exposed to a variety of literature from which they can choose for their independent reading; are supported and encouraged in their literacy efforts not only by me but also by their classmates; and leave my classroom with an arsenal of reading, writing, listening, speaking, and thinking strategies they can use in their content area classes.

Short Stories

Short stories are the backbone of my read-aloud program. With the explosion of quality short story anthologies aimed at middle school and young adult readers, there are enough short stories to please just about everybody—a kind of Ben & Jerry's for every literary palate. The only thing difficult about using short stories in a read-aloud program is keeping track of them, and I'll explain how I do that later in this chapter.

In discussing the recent evolution and trends of short stories, respected short story editor Donald R. Gallo (1998) explains why many of the classic short stories found in most textbooks often do not appeal to middle school readers. Gallo points out that although well-written, many time-honored short stories, such as Ernest Hemingway's "The Killers" and Jack London's "To Build a Fire," lack a teenage perspective. And although I believe like Gallo that there is a place in the curriculum for such stories, I don't believe they belong in most middle school classrooms filled with today's typical middle school readers.

Gallo suggests short stories that are likely to appeal to middle school students:

✓ Have characters the same age or slightly older than the students themselves

✓ Provide readers vicarious thrills (like the ones they get from scary stories)

✓ Be written from a teenager's perspective

✓ Deal with topics teens are concerned about or are related directly to their lives

Keeping the above criteria in mind, let me explain what I first do in my classroom with short stories and then how I continue to use short stories throughout the school year in my read-aloud program.

Peruse, Pick, Ponder, and Pencil

Although I begin my read-aloud program the very first class period I meet my students, I wait a few weeks into the school year before introducing my short story unit called "Peruse, Pick, Ponder and Pencil." To begin the unit, I review or teach the basic literary elements of character, theme, setting, plot, mood, and tone using a short story which I enlarge and put onto an overhead transparency. Next, I introduce the requirements of the unit, the required assignments, and the grading rubrics. Next, I model, by talking out loud, how I "Peruse" a collection of short stories by looking at each book's cover, at the categories (if the anthology is organized in this fashion), the story titles and the names of the authors. Next, I explain the reasons behind my "Pick" or choice of story, and then I read the story aloud, stopping to add my thoughts as I read. The third step is "Ponder," as I look at the variety of literature response activities that are required. These response activities come from my books *Better Than Book Reports* (Scholastic, 1992) and *25 Fun and Fabulous Literature Response Activities and Rubrics* (Scholastic, 2002). Although I use a variety of response activities depending upon the students in my classroom, I often use "Double-Nickel Stories" which requires students to summarize the plot and theme of the story using exactly 55 words, "Pertinent Plot Parts" which requires students to identify and prioritize significant plot events, "Fitting the Character to a T" which requires students to list the main characters' traits and provide examples from the text for support, "Sizing up the Setting" which requires students to select portions of the text to describe the setting and to draw a scene from the story, and "Cornering the Conflict" which requires students to identify the type of conflict in the story. Because I have explained these response activities earlier, during the "Ponder" portion of this demonstration, I model how I match the story to the activity. For example, if the story has an exciting plot, I choose the "Pertinent Plot Parts" activity; if the story has an intriguing main character, I choose "Fitting the Character to a T" and so forth. Finally, I explain to the students how I use "Pencil" to complete the activities so I can change and rearrange the information on the response sheets while I complete them. During the next several days, students "Peruse, Pick, Ponder, and Pencil" their way through the hundreds of short stories available to them via my classroom collection and a library cart laden with short story anthologies.

Matching Story to Reader

My job while students are working is to "match" students to stories, guide students to match the appropriate story to the most appropriate response activity, and crowd control. First, because independent reading is important in my classroom, I work hard to "match" the right book with the right reader, and I try to do the same with short stories. To make a "match," I ask the student the name of the best book s/he's ever read, what kind of "reading mood" s/he is in ("Are you in the mood for a scary story or a quiet, sad story?") and to compare the type of story s/he wants to read to another book or story s/he's read ("I want a story just like . . ."). Armed with this information, I make suggestions for the student. (Note: To help me remember the stories, I write keywords under each title on the table of contents page in my own books. As for the anthologies from the library, I try to keep a note card for each book with titles and keywords. In addition, I always ask students to recommend stories to me from new collections or from collections I'm not familiar with.) In addition to pointing students in a meaningful direction, I also help students match their story to the appropriate response activity. Since the activities mainly focus on plot, character, setting, theme, and conflict, I use a series of questions and prompts to help "tease out" the connection so the student can make a good match between story and response activity. Some questions I ask include:

- Was the story what you expected it to be? Why or why not?
- Describe the main character for me so I can "see" him, her, or it.
- Would you recommend this story to a friend? Why or why not?
- Was the setting unusual or did it play a significant part in the story? How?
- Describe the problem that had to be resolved in the story.
- Tell me what happens in this story.

My final responsibility while the students are working is crowd control. Each student is doing something different and while that is how I want this type of learning activity to be structured, it can lead to confusion. So if I see a student jumping up and running to the library cart or book shelf too often, I know s/he isn't "perusing" carefully enough: I play soft music to mask the noise of rustling papers so students can read; and I set aside time for students to stop reading and writing and move around the room to talk to each other about their stories because students are like the rest of us—when they finish reading something they really like, they want to tell someone about it!

Cataloging Suggestions

After the students and I have completed this unit, short stories become a regular part of our read-aloud routine throughout the school year, whether I read the story aloud, or whether the story is read as part of Readers Theater or part of a Musical Literature read-aloud. However, the only way I've been able to manage to keep short stories as part of my regular read-aloud routine is to use an organized system to keep track of them.

To be honest, I was driven to create a system to help me keep track of the short stories I was reading to my students, when one day one of my classes let me know that I had just introduced a story to them they had listened to twice before. They politely but firmly let me know they did not want to hear the story a third time and told me it was time for me "to read something different." I came to realize that I was lost in a sea of sticky-notes and couldn't keep up with what, when, and to whom I had read various stories. So I got organized, and I wish I could tell you that it felt good, but it was—and still is to some extent—work.

This is what I do:

- After I read a story, I decide which category to place it in.

- I fill out a note card for the story and put the note card in a file box I keep on my desk.

- When I plan each week's lesson, I pull the note cards of the stories I want to read and use them as book marks in the books in which the stories appear. I write the title of each of the stories in the Read-Aloud sections on my lesson plan sheets.

- I stack the books in a basket next to my stool in front of the room so I know where the books are when I need them.

- At the end of the week after the last read-aloud, I write the date I read the story on the appropriate place on the note card and return the card to the file box.

The categories I use to organize my short stories are fairly broad, and I use them to categorize the suggested stories I've included at the end of this chapter. However, many stories can fit into several categories so my system isn't flawless. I could cross-reference, but who has the time? After all, the time I spend on note cards, I could be reading. And I prefer reading to writing out note cards any day! The note cards aren't special, but I use a regular format like the one in Figure 8.1. A completed sample note card appears in Figure 8.2.

Category Heading: _____

Title of Short Story: _____

Author: _____

Title of Book where story can be found:

Length in pages: _____ Length in time: _____

Synopsis: _____

Special Notes: _____

Dates Used: _____

Figure 8.1   Short Story Cataloging Card

Category Heading *Humorous*

Title of Short Story " *Priscilla and The Wimps* "

Author *Richard Peck*

Title of Book Story can be found *Sixteen* (Gallo)

Length in pages *3 ¾* Length in time *Approx 5 minutes) with pre-reading explanation*

Synopsis: *A bully gets a valuable lesson*

Special Notes: *Use on 1st day of school. Explain Garden of Eden, extortion, Imagine a girl named Priscilla, fate*

Dates Used: *8/23/02   8/22/03*

Figure 8.2   Sample Short Story Cataloging Card

Student Responses

Of course I read aloud short stories for all of the reasons mentioned in chapter 1; however, when I read aloud a story, I want to take advantage of stories that are written specifically for middle school readers. I want to discover if and how the story connects to the listener. I want to discover if any sentences or phrases from the story are memorable enough to the listener that they are worthy enough to "collect" for future reference and repeating. I want to discover if the author has painted such a vivid "word picture" of a story's character or a specific scene or setting that a student can make a drawing of the character, scene, or setting. The three "discoveries" with which I challenge my students involve three different listening responsibilities. Two discoveries require students to listen to the read-alouds with a sticky-note and a pen or pencil handy, and the third discovery affords the student who likes to scribble and draw during read-alouds the opportunity to draw what s/he hears.

Before describing the three response activities, let me explain that I don't interrupt my read-alouds with a lot of questions, explanations, or opportunities for students to discuss the on-going reading. I know that others who champion read-alouds believe in stopping and letting elementary-age students respond during the read-aloud. (Beck & McKeown, 2001). However, I don't encourage my middle school students to do this. It's not that I don't want students to respond—I do. However, stopping too frequently interrupts the mood and tone of the story; and for some students, it can lead to confusion if discussion gets too far off topic. Also, too much discussion during an ongoing read-aloud can actually detract from comprehension if an especially vocal student offers predictions and story interpretations that confuse and frustrate other listeners.

Because I don't stop frequently during my read-alouds, I do a lot of preliminary discussion and explanation. I solicit prior knowledge from students, explain words that may be unfamiliar, and generally give a framework for comprehension by telling students what to listen for. Of course, if I see puzzled expressions on my students' faces, I stop and ask for questions; and I pause to let laughter die down or for students to react to an especially gross part of the story. These are natural, spontaneous reactions. However, the bottom line is, during read-alouds I don't "teach the book" as was suggested in a recent workshop I attended. To me, "teaching a book" during read-aloud time is not *affective* literacy education. To me, "teaching a book" is more appropriately done during guided reading instruction.

Make a Connection

Discovery One is a listening response I simply call "Make a Connection." While listening or during the reflection time after the read-aloud is completed, students write on a sticky note a connection they've made to the literature. The connection or connections, if the student makes more than one, can be categorized into three areas. Students make connections to the reading according to something they've read, something they've experienced, or something they know or remember. The student examples in Figure 8.3 were written when I read aloud *Sounder* by William H. Armstrong (HarperCollins, 1969).

Language Lifts

Discovery Two is a listening response I call "Language Lifts," which is a variation of sentence collecting (Speaker & Speaker, 1991). It is similar to "Make a

When the teacher talks
to the flower and said "that's OK
You'll grow back. It sounds like
what The Boy would say to Sounder.

Sounder

When I was young
I carried books
everywhere with
me like him.

Figure 8.3 Student Examples of "Make a Connection."

Connection" because students use sticky-notes and write during or immediately after the completion of the read-aloud. However, for "Language Lifts" students make a different kind of connection—a connection to a sentence or phrase that especially stands out or "strikes a chord" in the student. For example, when I read a book I put strips of removable highlighter tape over the sentences that are so well-written that I need to share them with someone at a later time. A case in point is when I read Avi's *Crispin: The Cross of Lead* (Hyperion, 2002), and I highlighted for future reference the following sentence from page 97: "Lose your sorrows, and you'll find your freedom." When I shared this sentence to demonstrate to students what a "language lift' was, I explained that this sentence struck me because of its simple truth. Sorrow, like a prison, traps people and restricts their freedom to enjoy life. Thus with "Language Lifts," students recall a sentence and record it on their sticky-note. (Note: Students will recall part of the sentence but may need to see the text in order to record the exact words of the sentence. If you have additional copies of the story that students used to follow along while you read, you can pass them around or else simply let students pass your book around to copy the exact text.)

See What I Hear

Discovery Three is called "See What I Hear." In this response, students sketch what they hear. In other words, they sketch a character, a scene, an object—anything they see from the description in the story. After all, a big part of comprehension is making a picture in your head.

For students who are artistic and for students who enjoy scribbling while listening, "See What I Hear" allows them to respond with their art rather than with written words. I explain to students that their sketch will not be judged as

Figure 8.4   "See What I Hear" Student Response to *A Long Way From Chi-cago* by Richard Peck.

an art project, but it needs to be more than "stick people" and must include details gleaned from the story's descriptive passages. Also, I tell students to "listen for" a certain descriptive passage or "listen for" the way in which the author describes a particular scene. In this way, I'm giving students cues so they can prepare themselves to listen even more closely to the story during those passages.

After the read-aloud is completed and after students have had time to reflect and draw or write their responses, I gather the sticky-notes and sketches and put some of them up on the board. I read a few and let students explain their responses if they wish. (Note: Sometimes a student will write "Do not read aloud" at the top of his or her sticky note, and I honor this request.) I enjoy the response or what I call the "Talk Time" part of the read-aloud because not only do I learn a lot about my students, but the activity also helps "build community" within the classroom.

Short Pieces

When I ask teachers why they don't read aloud to their students on a regular basis, their usual reply is lack of time. Too much curriculum to cover and not enough time. I know about having a lot of curriculum to cover, and I know about not having enough time. However, if you read chapter one carefully, you know that read-alouds can help you meet the requirements of your curriculum and help you meet standards. With that said, it is an academic fact that we teachers run out of classroom time. So when time is short, only a Short Piece for read-aloud will do.

I make it a point to collect, clip, and copy interesting short read-alouds that vary in length from a pithy quote to a two-page crime scene "you-solve-it" mystery. My "collection" of Short Pieces rests mainly in a wicker basket on the front table of my classroom. When time is short, I grab an article, note card, or book and quickly read aloud a selection. Short Pieces read-alouds are for those days when things took longer than expected or things took as long as expected and time is short. I read Short Pieces when I have a couple of minutes or even a couple of seconds before the bell rings, when I need to transition from one activity to another, or whenever I see the need to pull the students back into the mindset of being a "community of learners."

My collection of Short Pieces is eclectic, and yours should be also. I've included some titles to get you started, but one of the best sources for Short Pieces are the unusual stories that occasionally show up in newspapers and magazines. You know –the stories about letters that are finally delivered after being mailed 20 years prior. A note about keeping track of the Short Pieces you read. As I mentioned, I keep my stash in a basket. I read through the books and put a sticky-note on each Short Piece that is good enough to read aloud. If I grab a book to read, I turn to a page with a sticky-note on it, read the piece, and turn the sticky-note down. This indicates that I've read the piece so I don't repeat myself if I happen to grab the book again. At the end of the year, I bend the sticky-notes back up and I'm ready to go for the next year.

Reading aloud novels, short stories, and short pieces are wonderful ways to include read-alouds in your classroom. They represent the "traditional" literature formats that teachers have used. And nothing is wrong with tradition.

Resources

Novels

When Zachary Beaver Came to Town by Kimberly Willis Holt (Bt. Bound, 2001). When Zachary Beaver, "the fattest boy in the world," comes to town, Toby's life, as well as Zachary's life, change.

The Skin I'm In by Sharon G. Flake (Scholastic, 1998). Maleeka is picked on relentlessly. Her hair isn't right' her clothes aren't right, she's too skinny and her skin is too dark. Then Miss Saunders comes to teach at McClenton Middle School. Things get bad and then they get even worse. Eventually, however, Maleeka learns to be happy inside her own skin.

Give a Boy a Gun by Todd Strasser (Simon Pulse, 2002). This is a troubling story about boys, bullies, and guns told from the viewpoints of the students, parents, school administrators, and the shooters themselves.

The Shadow Club by Neal Shusterman (Dutton, 2002). Always second-best, seven "good" junior high students form a club to get even with the students who best them.

Among the Hidden by Margaret Peterson Haddix (Simon & Schuster, 1998). Luke is illegal. He is a third child living in hiding due to the government's two-children-per-family policy to combat widespread food shortages. Accidentally, Luke meets another third child, whose spirit and zest for life impress Luke. Her name is Jen, and she refuses to be "among the hidden."

Short Stories

Lots of books offer lists of short story collections, but I'm not going to do that to you. I used to look at those lists and think, "Where do I begin?" Instead, the stories listed below are some of my favorites from the collection of short story anthologies I have in my classroom. I've categorized each short story for you and identified the book in which you'll find it.

Entertaining Stories

"Priscilla and the Wimps" by Richard Peck (*Sixteen*)

"Shotgun Cheatham's Last Night Above Ground" by Richard Peck (*Chicago*)

"Duel Identities" by David Lubar (*Lost & Found*)

Creepy Stories

"The Doll" by Carol Ellis (*Thirteen*)

"The Binnacle Boy" by Paul Fleischman (*Graven Images*)

"The Caller" by Robert D. San Souci (*Thirteen Stories to Chill and Thrill*)

Self-Discovery

"Victor" by James Howe (*Birthday Surprises*)

"No-Guitar Blues" by Gary Soto (*Baseball in April*)

"My People" by Margaret Peterson Haddix (*Destination Unexpected*)

Unexpected Endings

"The Right Kind of House" by Henry Slesar (*Read if You Dare*)

"Battleground" by Stephen King (*Read if You Dare*)

"The Boy Next Door" by Ellen Emerson White (*Thirteen*)

Boy-Meets-Girl or Girl-Meets-Boy Stories

"Moonbeam Dawson and the Killer Bear" by Jean Davies Okimoto (*Connections*)

"Seventh Grade" by Gary Soto (*Baseball in April*)

"The Kiss in the Carryon Bag" by Richard Peck (*Destination Unexpected*)

Unfriendly Friendships

"On the Bridge" by Todd Strasser (*Visions*)

"Shortcut" by Nancy Werlin (*On the Fringe*)

"Mongoose" by Jerry Spinelli (*The Library Card*)

Teens in Danger

"Good Girl" by Marita Conlon-McKenna (*Thicker Than Water*)

"Golpe de Estado" by Dian Curtis Regan (*Shattered*)

"Echoes Down the Rails" by Kristi Holl (*But That's Another Story*)

Fairy Tale Twists

"As Good as Gold" by Vivian Vande Velde (*The Rumpelstiltskin Problem*)

"A Wolf at the Door" by Tanith Lee (*A Wolf at the Door*)

"Ahem" by Nancy Springer (*Ribbiting Tales*)

Science Fiction and Fantasy

"As True as She Wants It" by David Skinner (*Thundershine*)

"The Last Book in the Universe" by Rodman Philbrick (*Tomorrowland: Tales of Metakids*)

"*Skin*" *and Other Stories* by Roald Dahl (Puffin, 2000)

Short Story Collections

Thirteen Stories to Chill and Thrill by Robert D. San Souci (Cricket Books, 2003)

Baseball in April by Gary Soto (Harcourt, 1990)

Trapped! Cages of Mind and Body Edited by Lois Duncan (Simon & Schuster, 1998)

Visions Edited by Donald R. Gallo (Bantam, 1987)

Connections edited by Donald R. Gallo (Bantam, 1989)

On the Fringe edited by Donald R. Gallo (Dial, 2001)

Ribbiting Tales edited by Nancy Springer (Scholastic, 2000)

The Rumpelstiltskin Problem by Vivian Vande Velde (Scholastic, 2001)

A Long Way From Chicago by Richard Peck (Scholastic, 1997)

Read if You Dare (Millbrook Press, 1997)

The Library Card by Jerry Spinelli (Scholastic, 1997)

Lost & Found edited by M. Jerry and Helen S. Weiss (Tom Doherty Associates, 2000)

Tomorrowland edited by Michael Cart (Scholastic, 1999)

Graven Images by Paul Fleischman (HarperTrophy, 1982)

Destination Unexpected edited by Donald R. Gallo (CandleWick, 2003)

Sixteen edited by Donald R. Gallo (Bantam, 1984)

Thirteen edited by T. Pines (Scholastic, 1991)

Birthday Surprises edited by Johanna Hurwitz (Beech Tree, 1995)

A Wolf at the Door edited by Ellen Datlow and Terri Windling (Simon & Schuster, 2000)

Thicker Than Water edited by Gordon Snell (Delacorte, 2001)

Shattered edited by Jennifer Armstrong (Knopf, 2002)

But That's Another Story edited by Sandy Asher (Walker & Co., 1996)

"Skin" and Other Stories by Roald Dahl (Puffin, 2000)

Thundershine: Tales of Metakids by David Skinner (Simon & Schuster, 1999)

Short Pieces

Talking Walls by Margy Burns Knight (Tilbury House, 1992). Introduces listeners to famous walls such as Nelson Mandela's Prison Walls, the Vietnam Veterans Memorial, and the Western Wall in Jerusalem.

The Kid Who Invented the Trampoline by Don L. Wulffson (Dutton Children's Books, 2001). Brief explanations about how such things as ketchup and surfboards were invented.

Mistakes That Worked by Charlotte Foltz Jones (Doubleday, 1991). Brief descriptions of how mistakes led to the creation of such things as popsicles and Velcro.

We Were There, Too! Young People in U.S. History by Phillip Hoose (Farrar Straus Giroux, 2001). An incredibly diverse collection of brief stories that tell the role young people played in the history of the United States.

They Too Were Heroes: True Tales of Courageous Dogs by Joanne Mattern (Troll, 2002). True stories in which dogs come to the rescue.

Wacky Laws: Over 100 Ridiculous but Real Laws by Barbara Seuling (Scholastic, 1975). A list of strange laws that had a purpose at one time but sound ridiculous by today's standards.

Science: 150 Facts You Won't Believe! By Hugh Westrup (Trumpet, 1997). Interesting facts to boggle your students' minds like "snakes smell with their tongues."

Ten Thousand Children: True Stories Told by Children Who Escaped the Holocaust on the Kindertransport by Anne L. Fox and Eva Abraham-Podietz (Behrman House, 1999). True stories with updates as to where each individual is today and what s/he is doing.

References

Beck, I. L., & McKeown, M. G. (2001). Text talk: Capturing the benefits of read-aloud experiences for young children. *The Reading Teacher, 55* (1), 10–20.

Beers, K. (1998). Choosing not to read: Understanding why some middle schoolers just say no. In K. Beers, & B. G. Samuels (Eds). *Into focus: Understanding and creating middle school readers* (pp. 37–63). Norwood, MA: Christopher-Gordon.

Gallo, D. R. (1998). Short stories—Long overdue. In K. Beers & B. G. Samuels (Eds). *Into Focus: Understanding and creating middle school readers* (pp. 333–346). Norwood, MA: Christopher-Gordon.

Moen, C. (1992). *Better than book reports.* New York: Scholastic.

Moen, C. (2002). *25 Fun and fabulous literature response activities and rubrics.* New York: Scholastic.

Speaker, R. B., & Speaker P. R. (1991). Sentence collecting: Authentic literacy events in the classroom. *Journal of Reading, 35* (2), 92–95.

Final Thoughts:

A Baker's Dozen

For me, reading a professional book can be exhilarating. I get excited about trying out new ideas and activities because I never want to be bored or be boring in my classroom. At the same time, sometimes reading a professional book can make me feel guilty. I begin to think about all the suggestions the author has made and of all the things I'm not doing in my classroom. Then I say to myself, "Wait a minute! I can't work any harder or faster!" Then I take what I can and do what I can with the information presented.

I invite you and urge you to be guilt-free as you take what you want and can from this book. I wrote it for busy teachers like you and me. It won't fix every difficulty you may be having in your classroom—no one book or idea can. If you aren't able to take away some of the specific details and activities mentioned in the preceding chapters, I hope you take away the BIG IDEAS listed below so that at some future date the materials in this book will serve you well. Serving you well is the reason I wrote it!

BIG IDEA # 1

Traditional read-alouds are teacher-centered routines and performance readings are student-centered routines.

BIG IDEA # 2

Read-alouds and performance readings must be planned and purposeful like any other component of your lesson plan.

BIG IDEA # 3

Research supports the idea that teacher read-alouds and student performance readings can be used to teach reading skills such as comprehension, fluency, and vocabulary acquisition. In addition, read-alouds and performance readings are motivational and align with many state standards and the findings of the National Reading Panel whose report influenced the No Child Left Behind legislation.

BIG IDEA # 4

You can assess the suggested read-alouds and performance readings by using the graphic organizers and rubrics provided in this book.

BIG IDEA # 5

Readers Theater is a type of student performance reading that is enjoyed by a wide variety of students including "reluctant" or "dormant" readers who often think that Readers Theater "isn't really reading—it's fun!"

BIG IDEA # 6

Teacher read-alouds and/or student performance reading should be done on a daily basis.

BIG IDEA # 7

Performance Poetry is a type of student performance reading that enables students to physically, emotionally, and cognitively understand poetry.

BIG IDEA # 8

Storytelling is a type of performance reading that allows students to direct and to create their own versions of written stories. At the same time, storytelling also provides students with the opportunity to create their own mental images as they listen to their classmates' stories.

BIG IDEA # 9

Picture books can entertain, intrigue, and entice middle school students.

BIG IDEA # 10

If music goes so well with movies, why not with books, too? The benefit of using music with books is that the listener gets to create moving pictures on the white screen of his or her own mind.

BIG IDEA # 11

Nonfiction is not just for research but is an appropriate source of literature for read-alouds. Used with directed listening activities and student response organizers, informational texts can be used to teach not only the recognition of facts but also summarizing techniques, visual literacy, and vocabulary.

BIG IDEA # 12

Teacher read-alouds give students opportunities to make connections between the text and their first-hand experiences, their world knowledge, and their connection to other texts they've read. In addition, teacher read-alouds can be used to encourage students to listen for examples of well-written sentences and to make mental pictures as well as actual pictures (sketches) while they listen.

BIG IDEA #13

Cataloging your read-aloud and performance reading materials and activities can be somewhat time-consuming but not as time-consuming as searching, searching, searching for the stories, books, and music you want to use.

About the Author:

Christine Boardman Moen

As an avowed "reading warrior," Christine believes in teaching students to love to read—not just how to read. Because of her efforts to nurture the love of reading, she received the 2003 Illinois Council for Affective Reading Education's Reading Award. The strategies and activities published in her books come from the work she does with her own students in her own classroom.

She has presented workshops at local, state, national, and international literacy conferences and continues to share her ideas with teachers through district workshops and in-service training sessions.

Christine is the author of nine professional books for teachers and one children's book. In addition to her published books, Christine's many published articles have appeared in professional magazines and journals. She earned her M.A. Ed. from the University of Iowa. Her mantra is "Seek, Nurture, and Excite the reader inside every student!" She and her husband have a daughter who attends Purdue University and a son who attends Texas A&M.

Index